'It is very rare to discover original thinking which
lenge the conventional theory of team leadership, m
ment. David combines academic rigour and depth
the application of this new mental model in real bu
read for all Team Leaders, Managers and Team Me

— *Gina Lodge*, Chief Executive Officer, The Academy
of Executive Coaching

'We've been so conditioned to expect and to accept the value of traditional
team-working that it takes something like David Kesby's *Extra-Dependent
Teams* to break the spell. David's explanation of how most of us *actually*
work together presents a picture with which I instantly identified. Once
David has distinguished traditional team-working from extra-dependent
working, his advice on how to manage and lead in that context feels applied
and intuitive. The way in which he reframes the reality of how many of us
work in a networked world speaks to many of the challenges and opportunities of the modern workplace: lack of employee engagement, stubbornly
poor organizational performance and a struggle to deal effectively with ambiguity and complexity.'

— *Jonathan Norman*, Manager, Major
Projects Knowledge Hub

'A fascinating synthesis of the work on teams and communities of practice. It
will help managers benefit from key insights and approaches from both sides.
We especially appreciate the emphasis on the importance of identity—a central aspect of our learning theory that has not been embraced in business to
the same extent as communities of practice. If the reframing of communities
of practice as extra-dependent teams helps managers understand and lever-
age the nuances of their differences and complementarity with traditional
teams, David will have made a great contribution to the literature on organizations in the 21st century.'

— *Etienne and Beverly Wenger-Trayner*, co-authors of
Learning in Landscapes of Practice

Extra-Dependent Teams

Inter-Dependent Teams: people working together to achieve a common goal.

Extra-Dependent Teams: people learning together to develop a common practice.

Extra-Dependent Teams: Realising the Power of Similarity reframes the conventional mental model of teams into two complementary mental models of Extra-Dependent and Inter-Dependent Teams. Both types of team operate inside organisations today, but convention doesn't realise their difference. Extra-Dependent Teams are present in organisations because of their similarity – they do similar work in similar ways, but don't actually work together. People who lead them often feel like they are herding cats. Convention cites them as dysfunctional.

But cats don't herd. They are independent whilst all being the same. Realising this difference provides new ways of understanding and addressing the problems that convention can't overcome.

The reader will be introduced to the distinctness of Extra-Dependent Teams, their dynamics, how they perform, how they develop and how to lead them. Inspired by research on communities of practice and social identity, the book delivers an original and pragmatic approach to teams, being packed with examples, case studies, practical guidance and words of warning for managers and others about how to transform their Extra-Dependent Teams from peripheral problems into engines of innovation and growth.

David Kesby has over 20 years' experience of developing leaders and teams. He is Managing Director of Kesby & Co. Ltd, and an organisational coach.

Extra-Dependent Teams

Realising the Power of Similarity

David Kesby

Routledge
Taylor & Francis Group

LONDON AND NEW YORK

First published 2019
by Routledge
2 Park Square, Milton Park, Abingdon, Oxon OX14 4RN

and by Routledge
711 Third Avenue, New York, NY 10017

Routledge is an imprint of the Taylor & Francis Group, an informa business

British Library Cataloguing-in-Publication Data
A catalogue record for this book is available from the British Library

Library of Congress Cataloging-in-Publication Data
A catalog record has been requested for this book

ISBN: 978-1-138-10651-2 (hbk)
ISBN: 978-1-138-10653-6 (pbk)
ISBN: 978-1-315-10155-2 (ebk)

Typeset in Times New Roman
by codeMantra

For Natasha, Jamie and Matthew

Contents

Figures

Tables

Foreword

Peter Hawkins

> The number of people we will be employing in the next ten years will become less and less, due to robotics, artificial intelligence, digitalization and out-sourcing. However, the number of stakeholders we will need to effectively partner with will grow exponentially, both in number and complexity.
>
> CEO interviewed in Hawkins 2017b

For too long research and writing on teams has studied teams as closed bound-aried systems, looking at their internal relationship, dynamics and functioning. Managers and team coaches would work with teams with the assumption that if the team members related well together and had effective internal meetings and communication, they would become a high-performing team. Increasingly, the work of many researchers and writers in the field has started to debunk this myth (Wageman et al., 2008; Hackman, 2002, 2011a, 2011b; Katzenbach, 2012; Hawkins, 2011, 2014a, 2014b, 2017a, 2017b). Instead we should focus on how 'teams co-create value, with and for, all their stakeholders' (Hawkins, 2017a: 351) because the performance of any team is always contextual.

David Kesby's novel thinking on teams encourages us to further question the conventional model. By introducing adjacent research on communities of practice and social identity theory to existing team research, his plural mental model provides a refreshing perspective for managers and team coaches alike to appreciate dependencies outside of teams as well as inside. As such this book adds to the growing literature that helps us understand how teams are neces-sarily becoming more fluid, more networked and more focused on external con-necting as much as if not more than its internal relationships. Yet David's work also shows us new ways to foster internal relationships such that the essential external connections are not just with 'them', but instead with part of 'us'.

David shows how an increasing number of teams are comprised of mem-bers who rely more on external others to deliver performance than they do on their own team colleagues. He provides clear ways that teams can determine whether they are Inter-Dependent or Extra-Dependent Teams, drawing on Katzenbach and Smith's distinction between a work group and a 'real team' (Katzenbach and Smith, 1993 and Hawkins, 2011, 2017a). He therefore helps team members to identify their relationships with multiple teams within the system and shows the different approaches this calls for from both the team leader and the team members. Notably, he describes practical approaches for Extra-Dependent Teams to learn together to not only benefit themselves but also benefit the development and performance of their external stakeholders.

However, all teams are needing to focus on their wider networks (Katzenbach, 2012), their inter-team functioning and how they contribute effectively to becoming a team of teams across the wider organisation and business eco-system (Hawkins, 2017a, 2018; McChrystal et al., 2015; Fussell, 2017) and how they partner with other parts of the business value chain (Hawkins, 2017a: 202–5).

In a systemic perspective, as opposed to a systems perspective, every team is an Extra-Dependent Team, in the same way that every species is extra-dependent on its ecological niche, and we as Homo Sapiens ignore this at our peril. Every human organisation is a wholly owned subsidiary of the wider ecology, which can shut any system down at any time. This is why we need to move from team coaching, to systemic team coaching and then to eco-systemic team coaching, that focuses on the multiple nested systems that exist both within teams and which teams are sub-systems within.

This book makes an inventive contribution to the growing literature and research that encourages teams to increasingly focus externally when addressing their performance and development, to think 'future-back' and 'outside-in'.

References

Fussell, C (2017) *One Mission: How Leaders Build a Team of Teams*, Macmillan, London.

Hackman, J R (2002) *Leading Teams: Setting the Scene for Great Performance*, Harvard Business Press, Harvard, MA.

Hackman, J R (2011a) *Collaborative Intelligence: Using Teams to Solve Hard Problems*, Berrett-Koehler, San Francisco.

Hackman, J R (2011b) Six common misperceptions about teamwork, *Harvard Business Review*, http://blogs.hbr.org/cs/2011/06/six_common_misperceptions_abou

Hawkins, P (ed.) (2014) *Leadership Team Coaching in Practice*, Kogan Page, London.

Hawkins, P (2017a) *Leadership Team Coaching in Practice*, Kogan Page, London.

Hawkins, P (2017b) *Tomorrow's Leadership and the Necessary Revolution in Today's Leadership Development*, Henley Business School, Henley.

Katzenbach, J (2012) Look beyond the team, it is about the network, http://blogs.hbr.org/2012/03/look-beyond-the-team-its-about (accessed 1 April 2013).

Katzenbach, J and Smith, D (1993) *The Wisdom of Teams: Creating the High-Performance Organization*, Harvard Business School Press, Harvard, MA.

McChrystal, S, Collins, T, Silverman, D and Fussell, C (2015) *Team of Teams: New Rules of Engagement for a Complex World*, Penguin, New York.

Wageman, R, Nunes, D A, Burruss, J A and Hackman, J R (2008) *Senior Leadership Teams*, Harvard Business School Press, Harvard, MA.

Acknowledgements

This book is the result of over ten years of research, experimenting, reading and writing. Whilst it has at its core a new idea, it is nonetheless supported by many great works by writers that have inspired me to think differently about things over many years. Principal amongst these are Etienne Wenger, whose work on communities of practice is a core foundation in this book, and Alexander Haslam, Stephen Reicher and Michael Platow, whose pursuit of the application of social identity theory brought a whole new perspective on leadership for me.

But this book would not have come about if I had not had the chance to test out my thinking in real teams in real organisations doing real work. The main people I have to thank for this include Rob Walton, Andy Duffin, Matthew Hannaway, Wes Cadby, Vaughan Latter, Stephen Dean-Corke, Adrian Cooney, Julie Warriner, Paul Trow-Smith, Ryan Anderson, Martin Smith, Charlotte Jefferson, Louise Forrest, Dave Bull, Mary Rose Gavin and Sarah Diller. Most of these people spent over a year with me on and off, working alongside them, occasionally observing them, sometimes coaching, sometimes trying out new experiments. Their trust in me was vital to be able to share some of the stories within this book.

I would particularly like to thank Lotte Poole, Steve Harvey, Rebecca Benton, Mike Alsop, Amanda Bouch and Belinda Smith who joined me in setting up DidCOP in 2013 which gave me the opportunity to explore the dynamics between people who could learn together, but who didn't work together. Your enthusiasm for learning together really helped me road test some aspects that working with a separate team couldn't have. You even adopted the name DidCOP, a play on words combining community of practice and Didcot, the town in Oxfordshire where we met. Thank you for your encouragement to pursue my thinking.

Some other people stood by me at particular points in the development of my thinking. Ian Kersey gave me optimism by acknowledging the benefit of the idea in the very early days, as has Sam Hannis at various points since. Roderick Miller was the first person I had never met before who saw something in my ideas and enthusiastically championed them for me. Anita Wild was the person who helped me come up with the terms Inter-Dependent and Extra-Dependent Teams. Thanks Anita.

In more recent years I have been overwhelmed by the support and encouragement of the staff at the Academy of Executive Coaching who have embraced my ideas and started to work with them. In particular, I would like to thank Karen Smart, Jane Kirton and John Leary-Joyce, but it has been Gina Lodge who has done most to welcome my work into their everyday lives.

I would also like to take this opportunity to thank the Academy of Executive Coaching for their excellent development of me as an executive and team coach. In particular the Systemic Team Coaching Diploma in 2017 stretched my practice in developing both Inter-Dependent and Extra-Dependent Teams in a way that I couldn't have imagined. For that I have to thank the Faculty staff, John Leary-Joyce, Moira Nangle, Carlos Remotti Breton, Alan Taylor, and above all Dr Hilary Lines and Professor Peter Hawkins whose interest and wise words have kept me true.

I could not have made progress on this book without the trusted advice and support of two friends who guided me through the proposal stage for the book. Ginny Worsley was a real trusted adviser. Simon Taylor was that and so much more – he's a really great friend and has been for all of my life. I also thank Kristina Abbotts and Jonathan Norman who have supported me most closely during the publication phase of this book.

One person supported me from early on in my thinking. She was present at key moments as my ideas developed, encouraged my curiosity, and even sponsored my work with her clients. We have learned together, challenged each other, shared feedback, compared observations and even worked together to develop Extra-Dependent Teams. Belinda Smith, thank you for all your collaboration, your support, your trust and your friendship. It has been invaluable to me.

But my final words of thanks are to my wife, Natasha. She has been my rock, my true companion throughout my journey to this point. She is the best team mate anyone could ask for. Through her I appreciate the real power of teams, for I am so much better with her.

Part I

1 Herding cats

What if you herd cats?

Managing a team can be like 'herding cats'. I've heard it countless times from managers and team members alike. Cats are notoriously independent animals and unwilling to be herded. So the saying is used to describe teams made up of people who insist on working individually rather than together.

People say it a lot. I've heard it a lot. It must happen a lot. So what's going on?

The conventional answer is to make them a team – to herd them. Convention says, make them interdependent; make them work together. But what if convention is wrong? What if the reason why everyone insists on being independent is because they work independently from each other? Then what?

Convention doesn't have a clear answer to that. The problem with convention is the answer is to team. It's *always* to team. Even when the team never works together on the same work.

But what sort of teams might we be talking about? They would have to be teams of people who came under the same line manager, but didn't ever work together. Can any exist?

Yes, they exist. Sales people are set up like this. Also doctors, physiotherapists, product managers, project managers, risk managers, country managers, engineers, vicars, the list goes on. Within their line-managed teams, they all act like cats – because they are. They work independently from each other. Why? Because they all specialise in the same sort of work as each other and so when doing their work, they depend on people outside their own line-managed teams. Doctors work with nurses and other specialists, sales people work with administrators and others to process orders, whilst product managers work with everyone involved in developing and producing the product.

So if you manage a team who all do similar things and who do them independently of each other, what do you do to maximise the potential of that sort of team? Well, convention doesn't have an answer. It has an answer for people made up of differences who all need to work together to get things done. There are plenty of resources to help you manage a conventional team. But they don't really help address teams of cats because they don't recognise them as a different type of team, they only recognise them as dysfunctional.

This book recognises such teams as different. This book is able to do that because it uses two definitions of teams rather than the conventional one definition. The two definitions are distinct and both are purposeful. Both are steeped in research on teams in real organisations that improve and perform.

Having two definitions addresses a swath of problems affecting managers and organisations who continue to maintain that there is only one definition of team. This plural approach to team definition answers problems like employee engagement which is mostly driven by the relationship with the team manager; problems such as innovation, which is often limited to small numbers of people in organisations, rather than in the hands of all people in organisations; and problems such as hierarchy which slows change down as everyone waits for the level above to set their goals around which they must team together.

Many managers have been liberated by convention – they turn their underperforming or dysfunctional teams into the higher-performing, engaging and exciting place that they expect. But at the same time many managers have been let down by convention – their attempts lead to people pretending to be collaborative, or spend time collaborating only for the really important work of the team to be missed. The effort to team becomes temporary with everything eventually returning back to how it was. Yet on its return, the situation is worse because everyone knows they have failed in what seemed to be a relatively simple task – improving the team.

A true story

Steve took up a new position as manager of a team of training consultants in a medium-sized organisation. It was ironic, but all eight training consultants provided team-development services to a variety of different clients. Typically, the training consultants worked independently focusing their time with their respective clients. Their job was to understand the client's needs, design a solution that met that need and then deliver it. They rarely worked together and only conversed if they requested some past material or some ideas about what other people had done with other clients. It was easy to recognise that this team was a herd of cats.

Even so, prior to Steve's arrival the training consultants had got on pretty well without much management involvement. Their previous line manager was the managing director of the organisation who simply didn't have the time to pay attention to the team's needs. So they had effectively acted as a self-managed team, winning their work by supporting the sales people, coordinating the workload with project managers and liaising with clients to ensure that they got what they needed. The business had grown thanks to their work – time spent organising things with clients helped ensure the training was well planned and time spent with sales ensured that the best, most up-to-date case studies were being used to design and sell competitive solutions. The way the team was structured was a key driver of the organisation's success.

But for the consultants it was clear that the team didn't actually operate as a team 'should' – there was a lack of interaction as consultants might go for months without talking to each other, each one pursuing their own performance target in isolation of the others and with no particular focus on a team goal. The irony that their own team was the complete opposite of what they provided by way of team development to client teams was not lost on them and it left consultants feeling awkward with their clients and frustrated with the organisation. So when Steve joined the team in the newly created role of consultant team manager, there was a great deal of optimism that perhaps this was their chance to address these issues and create a real team – one similar to those they successfully developed with their clients.

Steve was recruited from within the company following a standard selection process and he was fully known and supported by the team. The initial optimism of having a dedicated line manager was reinforced when he quickly scheduled monthly meetings for all the team to get together. Such meetings would allow the team to break the long periods of isolation and help build cohesion. It would also be an opportunity to address important issues around how the team worked together towards a common goal.

At the first meeting the issue of 'team' was directly addressed. Using one of the models they used with their clients (Katzenbach and Smith, 1993), the consultants self-diagnosed that they were a 'working group' rather than a 'real team'. Steve was clear he wanted to create at least a 'real team' and perhaps go even better to become a 'high-performing team'. Core to this was working together more often and building on the diverse strengths within the team. As a result the team committed to the plan of meeting monthly and developing specialisms and new roles within the team based on individuals' strengths.

Yet, for all their expertise in developing teams, the consulting team gradually started to get *worse* rather than better. Promises to attend monthly meetings led to conflicts with client demands. Over the course of a few months, consultants started to drop out of the occasional meeting with the excuse that they had to prioritise client work over the work of the team. This then became more regular, until one meeting when even the manager didn't attend due to the need to prioritise clients over the team. The commitment to spend more time with each other inevitably meant that there was less time to deliver work to clients. Whilst it was frequently touted that consultants could help each other out, it was clear to each consultant that offering such support just ate into their precious time even more. There was tacit agreement not to ask for help so that no one would be asked. Even the new roles added pressure to the team. Two new team leaders would help with regular performance reviews and help plan individual development, and a new knowledge champion and quality manager would support the team in exploiting new knowledge and ensuring consistency of delivery. But whilst these new roles were complimentary on paper, they did much to add more demands to the consultants and in so doing, increased the pressure to deliver. As pressure to deliver mounted, so team meetings were missed and even less time was spent with each other. The new roles rapidly eroded with individuals in those roles reverting to consulting work – supporting new sales and designing and delivering training. The team started to miss its performance targets over a period of months which finally triggered redundancies for about half the team. What had been the conventional solution to the same old problem had made things worse.

What went wrong?

Convention might well explain that the team failed to see through on its commitments, or perhaps that the common goal wasn't compelling enough or that the team didn't work out a coherent approach to combining their specialisms. Convention might point the finger at the way that team meetings were held or the style of the leader or something going on in the market that meant the business lost its way.

In truth the team worked really effectively *before* the manager decided that the only way forward was to become a team. What went wrong was that convention refused to acknowledge that the team structure as a working group was both *legitimate and performing.* The working group didn't need to become a team, it needed to be better at being a working group. If convention hadn't been so single-minded then the reality of what made the team work could have been acknowledged and all the frustrations about the team could have been dealt with in an entirely different way.

If Steve had been aware that rather than there being one way of understanding and developing teams there were in fact two, then he might have had a choice about what to do differently. With this choice Steve would have noticed that his team didn't *need* to work together to perform and they didn't need to specialise. Indeed, they didn't really need a common goal for them to achieve high performance in combination with each other. If convention had encouraged Steve to acknowledge that the team *actually* only performed when working with other people *outside* the team, then the story might have been very different. But Steve was only doing what convention encourages all teams to do – work together to achieve a common goal.

Steve and his team are by no means alone in trying to make teams better, only to make them worse. J. Richard Hackman, the Edgar Pierce Professor of Social and Organizational Psychology at Harvard University and a leading expert on teams, says 'having a team is often worse than having no team at all' (Coutu, 2009). Similar heavyweights Jon R Katzenbach and Douglas K Smith, in their compelling work *The Wisdom of Teams* (1993), indicate that many teams are 'pseudo' in nature, in effect pretending to be a team, but without delivering the promised performance output. In pseudo teams, they say the sum of the whole is *less* than the potential of the individual parts.

They recognise that such teams are not uncommon. Indeed, there is plenty of evidence to suggest that teams don't perform as well as the promise of teams would have us believe. 'Considering all of the empirical evidence from field studies together, it does not appear that teams alone either consistently, or robustly, produce the gains in productivity that are reported anecdotally' (Allen and Hecht, 2004).

Should we therefore re-define teams? No, teams have been redefined enough. What hasn't happened is for the notion of *groups* to be defined. Some groups can perform and they can also be compelling places for people to belong in. But for us to open our minds to this idea, we must challenge convention.

Giving legitimacy to the unconventional

For all the different solutions to the problems of teams of the years, they have failed to address the underlying issues in many teams (Hay Group, 2001; Allen and Hecht, 2004; Coutu, 2008; West et al., 2015). Challenging convention doesn't mean reinventing how to herd, yet again. It is about understanding what to do if herding just isn't the answer. Then what?

What if Steve had been encouraged to see the team as it really was rather than how he and everyone else wanted it to be? What if Steve had acknowledged that what he managed wasn't ever going to be a conventional interdependent team with everyone in it working together towards a common goal? What if Steve had a name for this non-conventional team, so as to give it legitimacy? Then he might see the pointlessness of herding and perhaps stop shouting and flapping his arms about like it would make a difference – because in some teams it just doesn't.

The purpose of this book is to give legitimacy to teams of people who don't meet the conventional definition of a team, but who can still add tremendous value to organisations through bonding together. This book is about recognising how Steve's team *actually* worked and how; by leading it fundamentally differently, such teams can not only improve their performance, but be engaging places to belong in and even generate innovation that adds strategic advantage to organisations.

To give legitimacy to such a team we need to give them a name. They are called Extra-Dependent Teams. Their members are noted for their similarity rather than their differences, their members stand out as *not* working together but still reporting to the same line manager and their performance is a combination of individual effort rather than collaborating towards a common goal.

Extra-Dependent Teams

Extra-Dependent Teams are given that name because they are made up of members who depend on people *outside* of their team in order to perform.

This means when considered against the conventional model of teams they look dysfunctional. But actually they are entirely functional. This is because members in Extra-Dependent Teams do very similar work as each other and this is a defining feature of the team. They might all be engineers, in sales, project managers, vicars, matrons or in Steve's case training consultants. In each case, each team member's role is similar, as are their skills and the knowledge required.

Through the lens of convention a lot of the features of Extra-Dependent Teams are misdiagnosed as faults: working apart is seen as working in silos, lack of interdependency is seen as uncollaborative, and working only towards their individual goal is seen as not being a team player. When such teams are seen through an Extra-Dependent Team lens, they can be seen to be working extra-dependently with people outside the team, collaborating with their key stakeholders, real team players with those who most depend on them.

This book is for all those managers, like Steve, who are working with teams that convention sees as dysfunctional and then provides a single solution that doesn't work. It's a tall order to defy such an entrenched convention as teams. I only hope that what you read is as compelling an idea as it was to me when I first thought of it, and was then inspired to research it and experiment with it over the following ten years. My hope is that Extra-Dependent Teams are recognised for what they are, rather than what they are not, and that managers and team members are given different tools, techniques and solutions to generate the same ideal outcomes that are the aspiration of any team – engaging, fertile places where performance is valued and generates pride and joy.

The layout of this book

The book is in three parts. Part I consists of three chapters that explore the nature of Extra-Dependent Teams – how they are different from conventional teams, where the idea originates from and how they complement rather than compete with conventional teams. Part II, Chapters 4–9, then deals with Extra-Dependent Teams specifically: what goes on in them, how to manage and develop them as well as the implications for leadership. Part III is a reflection on the journey that has brought this book to publication. Here are some further details of each chapter.

Chapter 2, Schools of herding, further examines the research underlying the conventional notion of teams but also turns to the research that helps to recognise Extra-Dependent Teams. This research is on communities of practice – groups of people who all do similar things, identify with each other and who develop their practice through learning together. Whilst this chapter is relatively academic, an understanding of the two schools of thought presented will aid you in better connecting what makes Extra-Dependent Teams different, legitimate and real. As a result, subsequent chapters will be better appreciated.

Chapter 3, Inter-Dependent and Extra-Dependent Teams, positions a new plural mental model of understanding teams. The full distinction is presented between these two different types of teams, including clear definitions and distinctions. With this clarity, the chapter goes on to explore how numerous Extra-Dependent Teams are in organisations and how they complement Inter-Dependent Teams to help deliver organisational success.

Chapter 4, The bonding power of Extra-Dependent Teams, starts concentrating our attention on Extra-Dependent Teams. It starts with identifying what bonds the Extra-Dependent Team together and continues to explain how powerful this bond is. The importance of identity in teams is introduced and explored. This is a critical chapter which lays out some of the key terms involved in realising the power of Extra-Dependent Teams which are then used within subsequent chapters.

In Chapter 5, Extra-Dependent Team dynamics, the dynamics of Extra-Dependent Teams are explained very differently from Inter-Dependent Teams. Learning and identity is fundamental to how the dynamics work and this chapter introduces the concept of layers and trajectories for understanding interactions between members. Plotting the team members' layers and trajectories enables a manager to anticipate challenges and to start to take action to help the team flourish.

Chapter 6, Extra-Dependent Team management, discusses how too often team management focuses on the wrong mental model. This chapter highlights the pitfalls of applying the wrong mental model to an Extra-Dependent Team. But once a manager acknowledges the plural mental model, they can appreciate the bond and the dynamics in the team. Activities such as one-to-one meetings and whole-team meetings start to take on a different purpose. The role of manager is important and proactive. Chapter 6 explains what skills and techniques Extra-Dependent Team managers need to get it right.

In Chapter 7, Extra-Dependent Team performance, team performance is shown to be just as important in an Extra-Dependent Team as in an Inter-Dependent Team. But performance that is delivered outside the team needs to be managed differently. This chapter explains how managers need to step outside the team to manage performance and how managers can encourage their own team to better team with others. The chapter helps managers of Extra-Dependent Teams to see the importance of the team's performance within the wider organisation and to take practical steps to help everyone play their part for the organisation to perform.

Chapter 8, Extra-Dependent Team development, explores the importance of learning together. It draws on tried and tested techniques for developing people by liberating each other's knowledge and experience to combine it together for the improvement of all. There are case study examples of Extra-Dependent Team managers using different techniques to develop their teams. This chapter also highlights the prospects of innovation, how it can come about through the development of the team and how it can have strategic benefits for the wider organisation and beyond.

Chapter 9, Extra-Dependent Team leadership, grapples with the realities of what it takes to lead a team that simply doesn't allow for a conventional leadership style. This chapter explores the requirement of leaders to appreciate what it is to lead through crafting a common identity rather than a common goal and that being 'one of us' and 'doing it for us' bonds followers and leader together, enabling 'us' to bring meaningful benefit to the organisation and wider system.

Chapter 10, Reflection on practice, is reflective in nature and is personal to me as the author. I reflect on the various practices that I have been part of as I have developed the thinking, techniques and stories within this book. I feel it a fitting finish to the book that some of the pains and anxieties I experienced on my own journey have been explained and overcome through an appreciation of Extra-Dependent Teams. This chapter is an attempt to help you to connect more with me, the ideas and the early practice of Extra-Dependent Teams, so that perhaps you will find ways to adopt and adapt the learning here for the benefit of Extra-Dependent Teams that you are associated with.

Steve's team: a future fictitious scenario

Steve enters the team meeting as normal, a few minutes late. It doesn't matter too much as the rest of the team have started without him. The sharing of success always proves to be a winning starter at these meetings, particularly now that the team have learned to ask each other more searching questions about them. As Steve starts to listen to these engaging exchanges, he reflects on the positivity in the room. He finds it hard to believe that these people haven't seen much of each other over the last month, yet within minutes they are sharing deep learning with each other – learning that just isn't available anywhere else. He catches himself smiling. Steve knows that this meeting is already productive – helping people improve what they do and how they do it. Even if we finish this meeting in the next ten minutes, thinks Steve, it will have been worth it. Actually, they still have the rest of the day.

The topics on the agenda this month are around how people are using the new system, a report from Isha on the experiment she trialled last month and the normal round of challenges that everyone in the team brings to the meetings for everyone to explore together. This agenda had developed over the last few months, always for the better – a result of reviewing the learning process at the end of each meeting.

After the success sharing everyone takes it in turns to summarise their takeaways from the session and thank the person or persons they felt they had learned something from. After that it's Steve's turn to cover the new system. He starts by explaining how he proposes the review of the new system will happen. It won't be him taking centre stage. Instead, everyone will take it in turns to share something that they have found useful with the system and also something that they have found difficult. Steve explains that by sharing both, everyone will build confidence in their progress on the system whilst also helping each other with teething problems. It's accepted by everyone in the team as a good way for the whole team to learn together.

The session goes well and it remains upbeat yet relevant. Steve has learned that systems take time to learn and embed in individual and collective practice and that incremental exchange of real experiences helps everyone appreciate the benefits and overcome the pitfalls. With everyone working apart, time like this to help people feel like they're all in this together is crucial to the success of the new system. Steve sees this new system as another opportunity to build a sense of togetherness and consistency across the team – helping them to find the level ground for a good initial standard of working before encouraging them to raise the bar.

Isha's report is next and is deliberately short. The team have become adept at keeping reports to the bare essentials and then allowing the team to ask questions and explore the technique on trial with the presenter – the '20–80 rule' the team have begun to call it. When Dipta had done this first, Steve had felt short-changed. But what the team found was that the subsequent Q&A and discussion session had drawn everyone closer to what was involved in the experiment and also helped people to consider how they might incorporate such an approach into their own areas of responsibility. The discussion had gone so well that half the team started using the technique for themselves before the next meeting, with the remainder of the team gradually picking it up after that. The team had learned that short reports were best and Isha was following this approach – after all, it also meant Isha's preparation was minimised.

The part of the meeting that Steve always enjoyed most was the sharing of individual challenges. The team took it in turns to share a real challenge that they were experiencing within their areas – it could be anything about their work in the past month or even something coming up. Challenges were typically about something that went wrong that perhaps could have gone better – but how? Or challenges that were coming up that people didn't quite know how to approach and could run past the team for ideas and suggestions. The fact that each challenge was both unique and also very similar to other people's experiences still made Steve smile as he heard team members question, clarify, explore and make various suggestions. These discussions were so practical and covered so much in such a short time. People were always willing to share, knowing that the more they did so, the more support they got with their own challenge. Steve still had to pinch himself to realise how open and honest this team was with each other. It was so different to other teams he had been in.

Once again the challenges today had been far from trivial. Indeed, not everyone had had a chance to share, but the check-in with everyone at the end demonstrated that each person had very personal and practical actions and ideas to help them improve their own practice during the coming weeks.

By the end of the day everyone was exhausted, yet happy. The team had once again spent an intensive day learning from each other; learning together how to do their work better; the specific work that they did here in this organisation. During the meeting Dipta had remarked on how she had felt like the team had really bonded together over the eight months, even though the team probably saw less of each other since the new approach had been introduced. It had prompted a reflective discussion where everyone recognised how far they had come individually and collectively. Not only that, it was clear from the discussion that the wider organisation was starting to experience their combined impact and liked what they were doing. Their reputation in the wider organisation was improving.

It prompted Steve to make a note to himself to broaden out the discussions next time so that they accommodated more of the issues important to those people the team members dealt with. Doing this would help the team appreciate how they individually and collectively added value and what more could be done to ensure that they helped the organisation deliver its purpose. Steve felt closer now to contributing towards that than at any other time. He felt like the team was an important part of the organisation and that the organisation was starting to realise it.

Steve left the meeting knowing that each member was capable of achieving their individual objectives and that he was on course to meet the team target that the organisation expected him to deliver. Yet at no point had he asked anyone to share their performance results at that team meeting. He knew that the meetings were for the team to learn together and he was comforted that he would pick up performance at individual one to ones. He smiled wryly as he left the meeting because he also looked forward to such meetings as an opportunity to discuss performance progress and they helped him feel on top of his own performance. These one-to-one meetings had been transformed since he had learned some coaching skills. When before he had intervened, perhaps even taken over these performance discussions, he now asked lots of questions, prompting the team member to account for themselves, to keep in the driving seat and to deliver the performance. So long as he continued to coach in this way and keep the team members driving their own performance, Steve thought, he could find the energy and time to attend to the many other things that people outside the team expected of him.

And then it hit him. Tomorrow was his own line manager's team meeting and he would have to spend the evening preparing his numbers report to deliver to his manager in front of all his peers. Steve suddenly felt deflated as he reflected on the sheer effort it had taken at the last meeting to get through some relatively minor issues. It seemed that everything had to be perfect for these meetings. So tonight he'd make sure his figures were bulletproof; then the focus of the manager's attention would be someone else. But, he mused, why did these meetings have to be so exhausting? Why did everyone have to feel so defensive about their own areas? Why couldn't things be as progressive and trusting as it had been today with his own team?

References

Allen, N J and Hecht, T D (2004) The 'romance of teams': Toward an understanding of its psychological underpinnings and implications, *Journal of Occupational and Organizational Psychology*, 439–61.

Coutu, D (2008) Why some teams succeed (and so many don't), HBR.Org, 28 February, http://blogs.hbr.org/2008/02/why-some-teams-succeed-and-so-1/

Coutu, D (2009). Why teams don't work, HBR.Org, May, www.hbr.org/2009/05/why-teams-dont-work

Hay Group (2001) *Top Teams: Why Some Work and Some Do Not*, Hay Group, Philadelphia, PA.

Katzenbach, J and Smith, D (1993) *The Wisdom of Teams: Creating the High-Performance Organization*, Harvard Business School Press, Harvard, MA.

West, M, Armit, K, Loewenthal, L, Eckert, R, West, T and Lee, A (2015). Leadership and leadership development in healthcare: The evidence base, King's Fund, February, www.kingsfund.org.uk, www.kingsfund.org.uk/publications/leadership-and-leadership-development-health-care

2   Schools of herding

The reason why Steve tried to develop his team in a particular way was because it is conventional to recognise direct reports as a team. Convention expects direct reports to act like a team and when they don't act that way convention says that something is wrong. But convention is a mental model that can be challenged and re-created to better meet the needs of people's actual experience of the world.

Mental models

Mental models are 'deeply ingrained assumptions, generalizations, or even pictures and images that influence how we understand the world and how we take action' (Senge, 1990, p. 8). We use mental models in order to make sense of the world around us. They can be very helpful when the generalisations and assumptions match the experience we have. But if they don't match that experience, they can cause us deep problems.

An example of a mental model is the way we viewed the world's continents before 1960. It was widely believed that continents were static and had always been so. But there were features of the world that were hard to rationalise with this mental model. For instance, fossilised remains of tropical plants had been discovered in Antarctica and remains of species of creatures were found on separate continents. These were experiences that the mental model found difficult to explain. So the idea of land bridges was proposed to help justify how animals had travelled between continents. Academics argued that land bridges once connected the continents but had since been flooded or eroded away and hence they now couldn't be seen. But the evidence of such bridges was curiously difficult to find. The mental model that scientists were working with assumed the world's land masses had never moved and the hypotheses proposed were therefore limited to the boundaries of that mental model.

Other academics started to challenge this mental model by suggesting that the continents somehow drifted and in the 1960s the idea of plate tectonics was presented. This hypothesis, that the continents sit on vast plates that float on the molten core of the earth, was a completely new mental model of how we understood the world around us. But it immediately started to match the experience of the world around us. It not only helped to explain the distribution of fossil remains, but also why earthquakes and volcanoes occurred in some areas and not others, and it explained diverse geology such as the Himalayan mountains and oceanic trenches. It was such a simple way of understanding the world and helped explain so many things that were difficult to understand before that within a decade it had become part of main school curricula. The old mental model soon deteriorated. The new mental model was now pervasive and embedded.

Our understanding of teams is another such example of a mental model that we accept as a way of understanding the world around us. We use the mental model of teams to determine how things should be. It helps us understand why some teams 'work' and others don't. We use it to explain when things go well for us; or indeed when things don't. Because we share the same mental model it gives us a common language around which to make sense of the world. This language has been developed through popular culture such as watching sport or reading stories about adventures, and has subsequently been reinforced through academic research.

Formation of the team mental model

We are taught from a very young age to work together as a team and this is subsequently reinforced through popular culture such as sport, the military and stories of expeditionary feats. They all embed the notion that we should all aspire to work in teams. Sport is most prevalent for espousing the notion of teams. Children and adults play in hockey teams, netball teams, football teams, or perhaps rugby teams. Teams win, so everyone wants to be in a team. If we lose, we might be told that part of the reason was that we weren't working together as a team.

Expeditionary feats reinforce our understanding of and desire for a team; and they make for compelling stories that fix in our memories. Shackleton could not have escaped the treacherous conditions of the Antarctic if his men hadn't worked as a team. Nor could rowers crossing the Atlantic achieve their ultimate goal without acting as a team. Examples from the military further embed the notion of teams and how they are so important in achieving success. Many of these are fictional but no less compelling, such as the Three Musketeers, the A-Team or the Avengers.

Such an inescapable demonstration of what it means to be in a team forms a clear mental model that is extensively applied in organisations. The logic goes, if it's successful on the sports pitch, it must be successful at work. Organisations have therefore applied the mental model of teams 'sweepingly in organizations – to almost every situation, to solve every problem, and to achieve every goal' (Allen and Hecht, 2004, p. 440), even when it is far beyond any rational assessment of their usefulness. The team mental model leads to situations where employees 'try to present themselves, via speech and action, as people who are consistently quite keen on working in teams. After all, how can one employee say that they are not enthused about teams (or even a particular team) when teams are all the rage in organizations?' (Allen and Hecht, 2004, p. 454). The mental model creates an accepted convention where employees, managers, trainers and academics together form a value chain that all work with the same mental model of teams – even when the assumptions of the mental model contrast with our real-world experience.

Employees are at the base of the mental model value chain. The real-world experience for employees is that what they believe ought to be a team doesn't actually work like a team. Their manager might talk like they want a team, but they certainly don't act like it's a team. Research by Gallup indicates that about half of people quit their *bosses*, not their jobs (Weber, 2015). It's indicative of an engagement issue that the mental model of teams is supposed to overcome. For the employee, the mental model is easy to create in reality, so why doesn't the manager do it? Are they stupid or selfish? Either way, it means the employee leaves a job and abandons a bunch of colleagues that appeared to have so much potential together. The irony of this situation is that managers also want teams.

Organisations are constantly demanding managers to achieve more with less. They want more productivity, output, widgets, efficiency, effectiveness or whatever, all for less money, time and people. Like employees, managers also recognise that when they win, sports teams, military teams and adventurous teams achieve more than the sum of their parts. The conventional mental model of teams therefore provides a relatively straightforward way of solving the problem: teams promise a way forward for doing more with less. But research consistently indicates that managers just don't deliver the team as promised in the mental model (Robbins and Finley, 2000; Hackman and Wageman, 2001; Wageman et al., 2008; Allen and Hecht, 2004; West et al., 2015). The generalised conclusion is that around half of teams don't actually work in the way the conventional mental model would have us believe. So why doesn't someone do something about this? Well, people inside and outside of organisations do try to do something about this. They are trainers, human resource developers or consultants. They sit inside and outside of organisations and they attempt to address the deficiency in how teams are managed.

The many HR developers, trainers or consultants trying to address this team issue are joined by an army of over 12,000 training providers in the UK alone who will provide team-related[1] training services (National Institute of Adult Continuing Education, 2009). They are all geared up to provide clear lessons on how best to manage teams. They assess the problem, design solutions to the problem and deliver the training.[2] This is precisely the area in which Steve's team worked in Chapter 1. But what gives these trainers the right to tell managers how to do things? Well, in the case of Steve's team they all had some experience in management and teams themselves. But that was not enough to make managers turn to them for advice. Trainers needed to depend on leading academics in the field.

Academics are constantly researching, surveying and studying teams to understand how to address the issues in teams because the issues appear to be perpetual. Articles have titles such as 'Why teams fail', 'Highly effective teams' or 'The truth about teams'. The academics form the top of a value chain that feeds the conventional mental model of teams: academics who research teams that look and act like a team should, then write the books that fuel the trainers who train the managers who manage the teams. Academics then study these teams. They refine the conventional mental model of teams in an attempt to work out why cats don't herd and what can be done to ensure that they do. Together, the academics represent a school of thought that I will call the Team School.

The Team School

Heading up the Team School are authors Jon Katzenbach and Douglas Smith. Their seminal book *The Wisdom of Teams* gave both academic rigour and clear thought to the notion of teams in organisations. Having studied hundreds of teams, they defined them as: 'A small number of people with complementary skills who are committed to a common purpose, performance goals, and approach for which they hold themselves mutually accountable' (Katzenbach and Smith, 1993, p. 45).

This definition is still widely used decades later by training providers and other leading academics on teams (Clutterbuck, 2007; Hawkins, 2014). But if you ask a manager how *they* would define a team, they typically answer, 'a group of people all working together to achieve a common goal'. It's a simpler version of Katzenbach and Smith's yet still embodies the fundamental lessons about teams as espoused by the Team School. These factors form the conventional mental model of teams and include:

- teams are superior to groups;
- teams combine difference;
- teams are interdependent;
- teams have a common goal;
- teams have mutual accountability; and
- teams should be universal.

Teams are superior to groups

The core message within *The Wisdom of Teams* (Katzenbach and Smith, 1993) is that teams will almost always outperform a group. Groups are looked down on as individuals working as a single part of a process, in a silo or in a mechanistic way. The superiority of teams over groups is most clearly made through the Team Performance Curve, which is a simple graph that shows a working group achieving lower performance impact than either a real team or a high-performing team. The authors define a working group as having no significant performance need or opportunity that would require it to become a team whilst a *real* team meets the definition as cited above. Indeed, some teams can even significantly outperform peer teams. These are what the authors define as high-performing teams. Whether you achieve real team status or high-performing team status, the authors' point is clear – teams are better than groups.

The Team School argues that teams are better than groups because they achieve more than the sum of their parts. For Richard Hackman and Ruth Wageman (2001), teams are able to achieve 'something that could only be accomplished together'. Groups on the other hand simply can't achieve the same sort of performance level. It's a point reiterated in countless books on teams, teamwork, team development and leading teams. Many of these books cite the grandfather of the Team School, Bruce Tuckman, who coined the development stages, Forming, Storming, Norming and Performing (Tuckman, 1965). Such stages have been used by trainers and managers alike to clearly distinguish that groups fail to progress from the Forming or Storming stages and that only those that progress through to Norming or Performing can be considered teams. The superiority of teams therefore is directly linked to superior performance. But other factors are also important to the Team School.

Teams combine difference

The importance of combining difference in teams is what brings about higher performance according to the Team School. Katzenbach and Smith argue that 'Teams outperform individuals acting alone or in larger organisational groupings, especially when performance requires multiple skills, judgements, and experiences' (Katzenbach and Smith, 1993, p. 9). This is mirrored by Wageman et al. who state, 'the presence of diverse viewpoints has been shown to significantly increase a team's creativity and decrease the likelihood that the team will congenially make plans or decisions that turn out to be fiascos' (Wageman et al., 2008, p. 83). The work by Meredith Belbin on team roles identified nine behaviour types that helped groups to achieve as teams by using difference as strength (Belbin, 2004). Other indicators of difference between people in teams have also found voice within the Team School. So it is that the Myers-Briggs Type Indicator (Myers and Briggs Foundation, 2017) proves to be a popular tool used by consultants to highlight personality differences and to show how such differences can clash or complement people within teams (Lencioni, 2002). The Team School is clear and consistent that finding and combining difference is essential for teams to be successful.

Teams are interdependent

Difference is only important to the Team School when it creates interdependency. People with different strengths need to depend on each other and through doing so, the team achieves. For Hackman and Wageman, a team demands 'a high level of interdependency among its members' (Hackman and Wageman, 2001, p. 4), whilst Katzenbach and Smith describe this interdependency as commitment towards each other. Without it the team is no more than a group of individuals. Interdependency therefore requires people to do different things in order to work well together. Teams seek to ensure that everyone knows the unique part they need to play in order that together they can achieve the common goal.

Teams have a common goal

One indisputable feature of the Team School is the belief that teams have common goals; 'no team arises without a performance challenge that is meaningful to those involved' (Katzenbach and Smith, 1993, p. 12). For Hackman and Wageman it's 'a collective task' (Hackman and Wageman, 2001, p. 4) and for Lencioni it's 'an unrelenting focus on specific objectives' (Lencioni, 2002, p. 216) that are collective for all rather than specific for individuals. For the Team School, the common goal is what brings the team together. It is also the true measure of performance and the unique value that the team can provide. The common goal is what the team can hold itself mutually accountable for.

Teams have mutual accountability

Katzenbach and Smith make clear that they expect team members to 'hold themselves mutually accountable' (Katzenbach and Smith, 1993). Mutual accountability is vital to the Team School as it's what gives the team a sense of collective success; and indeed failure. If there were no mutual accountability, *individuals* within the team would claim credit and any sense of the team would collapse. Mutual accountability is evidenced when a Grand Prix driver wins a race and immediately thanks the pit crew or when the football team that wins a championship all stand together on the podium to lift the cup.

Lencioni highlights the avoidance of accountability as a key dysfunction in teams. For him and the Team School, mutual accountability pre-dates achieving the common goal. It starts much earlier, at the point of decisions and early action. 'The essence of this dysfunction is the unwillingness of team members to tolerate the interpersonal discomfort that accompanies calling a peer on his or her behaviour and the more general tendency to avoid difficult conversations' (Lencioni, 2002, p. 212).

The Team School paints a clear and compelling picture of what makes teams work. It also means that anything less than this is intolerable, underperforming, dysfunctional. These words are then used to distinguish teams from groups.

Teams should be universal

Whilst the Team School acknowledges that groups could have their place, their clear message is that the superiority of teams means that teams should be the preferred ambition of any group:

> We believe that teams – real teams, not just groups that management calls 'teams' – should be the basic unit of performance for most organisations, regardless of size.
>
> (Katzenbach and Smith, 1993, p. 15)

> The conditions we discuss in this book are valuable for any kind of task-performing team.
>
> (Wageman et al., 2008, p. 15)

> Organizations fail to achieve teamwork because they unknowingly fall prey to... natural but dangerous pitfalls.
>
> (Lencioni, 2002, p. 187)

The benefits of the universality of teams has more recently been elaborated by General Stanley McChrystal et al. in *Team of Teams* (McChrystal et al., 2015). The book promotes the notion that teams provide the solution to complexity for the 21st century. It is the essence of what it is to champion the Team School. Not only does it use academic sources to explain its point, it also returns to one of the foundations of the conventional mental model of teams – the military. For the Team School it is all about how the herding is done. If the herding is done well, the cats will herd.

When herding goes wrong

All mental models need to survive testing against reality. If we experience evidence that contravenes the mental model, we disbelieve it and we seek to amend the mental model. This is what happened with plate tectonics. The interesting thing about the Team School is that it has found strong evidence that teams don't work. For instance, Richard Hackman has found that 'work teams cluster at opposite ends of the success continuum. Many function beautifully; many others fail miserably. Few are in the middle' (Harvard Management Update, 2008). It mirrors work by Ruth Wageman that shows that over 40 per cent of senior leadership teams have poor effectiveness (Wageman et al., 2008). Similarly a recent national staff survey within the NHS revealed that most NHS staff (91 per cent) report working in a team. Yet follow-up questions intended to test for the existence of basic elements of team work (team objectives, interdependent working, regular meetings) revealed only around 40 per cent of staff report working in teams (West et al., 2015, p. 6).

The reason why people refer to managing their team as 'like herding cats' is because this continues to be the case. The metaphor of herding cats is a reality. It seems that the conventional mental model sustained by the Team School insists on more and better ways to herd. When a manager uses these team solutions with direct reports and it works, then great. The mental model is proven – again. But if the cats just won't be herded, then the Team School has little advice except to learn to do the herding differently. There appears to be no alternative.

No choice

Choose to team and succeed; or choose to group and fail. Of course, it's no choice. So what do managers do? They start with what is easiest. They refer to their direct reports as a team. It really doesn't matter if they act like a team, or meet the definition of a team; managers call them a team because to do anything else is to invite ridicule. This linguistic change is reinforced through the organisational routines of management such as 'team meetings' that talk about 'team goals', which might then lead to a 'team bonus' if achieved. But it's only a linguistic change and doesn't mean that the team is *actually* a team in the way the Team School promotes.

This is where things start to get confusing because of the imprecise language being used. Everything soon becomes a team, even when it is not. The research by West et al. (2015) that highlighted the number of people in the NHS who said they were in a team but who really weren't highlights the possibilities of confusion. And in my work as a consultant and executive coach, I often hear managers declare, 'the problem is, my team isn't a team!' To me, it's evidence that the conventional mental model of teams has become the solution to everything and when that happens the true value of the Team School can be too easily lost. In *The Lego Movie* there is a song that mocks the idealisation of teams. It's called *Everything is Awesome*:

> Everything is awesome
> Everything is cool when you're part of a team
> Everything is awesome, when we're living our dream.
>
> (Lord and Miller, 2014)

Listening to the song makes me smile because it sounds so familiar within organisations. But it also causes me frustration because I know how valuable teams can be. I have been in teams that have been high performing. I have worked hard to turn around teams that were dysfunctional and used the Team School mental model, tools and techniques to do so. So I'm all for herding – when it is appropriate. But where I depart from the mental model of the Team School is the assumption that everything can be a team; that every group can only improve performance *by becoming a team*.

But the Team School thinking is not the only way to improve performance in groups. Indeed, there is evidence of this in the work of the grandfather of the Team School. It seems the foundations of the Team School are not as secure as many people make out.

Seeing what you want to see?

The Team School has become so dominant in organisations over several decades that any groups that perform are believed to represent a team – even when they do not. Bruce Tuckman's (1965) work remains a core tool to help explain how teams develop. David Clutterbuck (2007) calls Tuckman's work 'the rubric' for team development, whilst Goffee and Jones (2006) use it as a tool for leaders to transform groups into teams. It constitutes the base material for any manager learning about teams, not least because its clear pathway to improvement is both simple and rhyming, so it's memorable. I have heard it referred to by people who have the least knowledge of the Team School. It also appears to underpin the very essence of the Team School. It shouldn't go unnoticed that there are great similarities between Tuckman's stages of development and the Team Performance Curve of Katzenbach and Smith. Both start at a relatively functional level (Forming/Working Group), before going through a period of confusion (Storming/Pseudo Team), before returning to the original level (Norming/Potential Team) and then progressing to something much more effective (Performing/Real Team). Tuckman's research is a clear early influence on the mental model developed by the Team School.

So it should come as a complete surprise to anybody wedded to the Team School mental model that Tuckman's research was based on secondary research on '50 articles, many of which were psychoanalytic studies of therapy or Tgroups' (Tuckman, 1965). Tuckman explained that a therapy group's main task was to help individuals better deal with their personal problems and that the goal of such groups is *individual* adjustment. For such a group to be described as a team is really quite a leap of faith. Similarly, in T-Groups (human relations training groups) the goal is interpersonal sensitivity with the task being simply to help *individuals* interact with one another in a more productive, less defensive manner. Therapy and T-Groups would not be what the Team School had in mind when defining what a team is. It can't even be said that the Performing stage was when the group somehow became a team. Their very nature and purpose would never achieve the status of team in the eyes of the Team School. Yet Tuckman recognised that, even though they were only ever a group, they could still develop and perform. Tuckman's paper makes clear what he was interested in. It was entitled, 'Developmental sequence in small groups' (1965). It's ironic that such a foundation of the Team School only uses the word 'team' once in his paper, and only then when referring to *another* academic source.

Are we to ignore Tuckman's work as an inconvenient truth? Those who romanticise teams might choose to do so. Instead, I would prefer to recognise that Tuckman demonstrates that performance is possible in groups that just aren't teams. Teams are therefore not the only answer.

This provides us with the possibility of considering an alternative to teams – to consider a different solution to disengagement and poor performance. Perhaps such an alternative might help address the ineffective teams that the Team School consistently doesn't seem to address? If Bruce Tuckman could find that therapy and T-groups can perform, then the Team School solution does not have to be universal. But what other way is there?

The communities of practice school

Communities of practice were first 'discovered' in the early 1990s, but even now they remain scarcely known, mainly because of the dominant mental model of the Team School. Jean Lave and Etienne Wenger first coined the phrase 'community of practice' in their book about situated learning (Lave and Wenger, 1991). They were interested in how people developed together. Their initial interest was in apprenticeships of all different kinds and they studied research on groups as diverse as butchers in US supermarkets, US Navy quartermasters, Yucatec Mayan midwives in Mexico and Vai and Gola tailors in Liberia. Their analysis and conclusions identified that people learned through participation within a community of people that represented the particular practice. The practice wasn't just the work being done, it included the place in which it was done, the artefacts involved, the relational dynamics between master and apprentice and the nature of what was learned.

Lave and Wenger called these groups communities of practice because they involved the dynamics between people (a community) who all did the same sort of thing (a practice) whilst all benefitting from each other's participation. In effect, everyone was learning together in pursuit of a shared practice. They saw learning as a social process which required everyone involved to be an active and legitimate participant, including the master in the master–apprentice relationship. To Lave and Wenger, learning wasn't simply a cognitive state of knowing, it required competence to do something like singing in tune, fixing machines or delivering babies. In doing so, *knowing* couldn't be a passive condition but instead had to be an act of participation in place and practice, the experience of which people drew meaning from. Meaning, they see, is the ultimate production of learning.

Clearly they were paying close attention to groups that were very different from those being paid attention to by the Team School. Whether or not any of these communities of practice could be described as a group or team by the Team School, the Community of Practice School was starting to see certain groups in particular ways; to see *commonalities* in groups that might otherwise be seen as diverse and unalike. Yet productive outputs came from these communities of practice, be it clothes from a Gola tailor, quality cuts of meat from a butcher or healthy mothers and babies from a Mayan midwife. Clearly, such communities of practice could be sustainable places to work, improve and perform.

Wenger went on to develop the idea within organisations by studying claims processors within an insurance company (Wenger, 1998). Whilst the claims processors sat together when they worked, they didn't actually need each other to do their claims-processing work. The claimant and the service provider (i.e. whoever was providing the service being claimed) were the main people that the claims processors interacted with. Even so, Wenger found that such workers established a strong sense of cohesion between each other as they shared their understanding of the work they each did, learned together and gradually built their shared practice.

Distinguishing communities of practice from teams

To help people understand what Communities of Practice are, Wenger contrasts them with teams. 'A community of practice is a different kind of entity than, say, a task force or a team' (Wenger, 1998, p. 96). As with the Team School, Wenger sees, 'the essence of a team [as] a set of interdependent tasks that contribute to a predefined, shared objective' (Wenger et al., 2002, p. 43). He then differentiates communities of practice by explaining that whilst teams have a common goal, communities of practice share an interest in a particular territory of knowledge and are defined by their fundamental commitment to exploring this territory and to developing and sharing the relevant knowledge. Indeed, the more the Community of Practice School has applied thinking to organisations, the more emphasis they have put on how distinct communities of practice are from teams.[3] For the Community of Practice School, therefore, teams have interdependent tasks whilst communities of practice are connected by interdependent knowledge.

This differentiation is made even more pronounced by Richard McDermott (McDermott and Archibald, 2010), who argues that communities of practice are informal networks that fit *between* teams in the organisation. Crucially, people in a community of practice, 'don't necessarily work together' (Wenger et al., 2002, p. 4), a clear distinction from teams, yet 'they meet because they find value in their interactions' (p. 4). As they spend time together, they typically share information, insights and advice, ponder common issues, solve mutual problems, create new tools, standards or approaches or simply develop a tacit understanding that they share together. Through this process they socially construct the knowledge of their shared practice, become informally bound together through the value they accrue from each other, build a sense of belonging and over time even develop a strong sense of common identity. To the Community of Practice School they constitute 'a new vehicle for collaboration *distinct from work-based teams*' (Hughes et al., 2007, p. 2., my emphasis).

Communities of practice are an integral part of our daily lives. They are so informal and so pervasive that they rarely come to explicit focus, but for the same reasons they are also quite familiar. As Wenger says, 'although the term may be new, the experience is not' (Wenger, 1998, p. 7). We participate in communities of practice in formal and informal ways. In our formative years, we participate in a community of practice in the classroom – learning together. We informally participate in a community of practice when we become a parent and discuss parenting with other parents – trying to make sense of how to do parenting well. More formally, we participate in a community of practice in our professional lives, learning our profession with many other people, some of whom we know and many of whom we don't, yet as professionals in the same field we are all part of the same community of practice. Together we individually and collectively develop so that we can be better in our work and achieve more.

Communities of practice are clearly very different from teams, yet still generate improved performance. Whilst teams use difference to work collaboratively together, communities of practice are based on similarity and don't need to work together – but they do need to collaborate together to learn.

Collaborative learning

One of the most powerful and consistent approaches to collaborative learning was first developed by Reg Revans after the Second World War. It pre-dates the discovery of communities of practice, but Revans is very much in the Communities of Practice School of thinking. He researched, experimented and proved that people who learn together, but don't work together, can have profoundly beneficial effects on each other. Revans called this collaborative learning *action learning*.

Action learning is typically arranged as programmes of learning outside of the normal organisational structure. It involves groups of managers sharing challenges and learning with and from each other. As with communities of practice, similarity was important for Revans. 'Action learning must seek the means of improvement from within, indeed, from the common task' (Revans, 1982, p. 283). Revans explains that during action learning:

> Subjects learn with and from each other by mutual support, advice and criticism during their attacks upon real problems, intendedly to be solved in whole or in part. The learning achieved is not so much an acquaintance with new factual knowledge nor technical art conveyed by some authority such as an expert or a teacher (although such fresh acquaintance is not ruled out), as it is the more appropriate use, by reinterpretation, of the subject's existing knowledge, including his recollections of past lived experiences. This reinterpretation is a social process, carried on among two or more learners who examine afresh many ideas that they would otherwise have continued to take for granted, however false or misconceived.
>
> (Revans, 1982, p. 627)

Action learning is, to all intents and purposes, a formalised community of practice. People with the same practice are brought together in organisations to deliberately learn together so that they can individually improve through the process of collaborative learning. The benefits of such groups have been researched by the Community of Practice School. Communities of practice can generate deep learning together not only to improve performance, but also to create new knowledge that can in turn lead to innovation which has strategic value (Wenger et al., 2002; McDermott and Archibald, 2010).

The work of the Communities of Practice School demonstrate that communities of practice are not only important engines of performance improvement within organisations, they are also places for people to collaborate, overcome problems, even enjoy a sense of belonging. So why aren't they more widely known about?

The relegation of the Community of Practice School

I believe there are a number of reasons why the work and benefits offered by the Community of Practice School are not more widely known or adopted. Firstly, the 'noise' generated by the Team School through the value chain of academics, trainers, managers and employees has led the Communities of Practice School to be overlooked as a mainstream option and pushed very much to the periphery. Secondly, due to the polarised choice that the Team School prescribes between 'group' and 'team', a third option as offered by the Community of Practice School not only blurs the clarity of this choice, but perhaps also undermines the Team School's raison d'être. Thirdly, the Community of Practice School is perhaps as wedded to the conventional mental model of teams as the Team School is, in that they cannot see any circumstances by which a community of practice might actually exist *within* the formal structure of an organisation. It appears they see this as the exclusive territory of the Team School. They too assume that all direct reports in organisations should become teams. The Community of Practice School therefore rules itself out of being able to provide a solution to any problems associated with teams in organisations.

But is this really the case? Might there be circumstances within which a manager and their line reports better match a community of practice rather than a team? The Team School justifies its need based on the continued existence of underperforming teams, yet one solution has no material impact to the proportion of teams becoming effective. The polarised choice of team versus group just isn't delivering the goods. We need to break out of the conventional mental model and recognise that there is another way to view the development of teams in organisations: through communities of practice. Communities of practice and teams can both be used to develop collective performance in organisations.

This is possible because both schools of thought are, at their core, social phenomena. Both teams and communities of practice naturally occur and are observable within our world. Teams have been around since sport, expeditions and the military have been operating (millennia) and so the Team

School is simply describing what they notice happens when such teams of difference perform within organisations. Likewise, communities of practice date back as far as the start of tailoring, butchering, midwifery and even parenting. The Community of Practice School has simply described what it sees happen when such groups of similarity perform inside and outside organisations.

Teams and communities of practice therefore both pre-date any modern construction of organisation. Yet, as social phenomena they continue to be ever present within our organisational structures because, whether we appreciate it or not, both phenomena are functional. Both achieve performance improvements. Both enable people to feel good about their work. Both enable people to appreciate their value in the world.

And whether we notice or not, both are currently occurring within organisations. Both form structured teams. Some teams are of difference and some teams are of similarity in organisations. The sooner we notice them for what they naturally are, either teams or communities of practice, the sooner we can use the most appropriate approaches to help realise their potential. Both schools of thought are beneficial. Teams are not the universal solution.

A new plural mental model of teams

There needs to be a new mental model of teams created. One that incorporates the compelling solutions that both schools of thought offer. Such a mental model would provide a new choice to managers, one that wasn't simply a prescriptive singular solution in all cases. Such a new mental model would accept a *plural* approach using the potency offered by both schools of thought. This mental model would rely on the *description* of the team phenomena – how it really *is* – rather than the *prescription* handed out irrespective of the team's conditions.

The typology of mental models in Figure 2.1 captures how this new plural mental model is an advancement on the prescriptive conventional model, which in turn is an advancement on having no mental model.

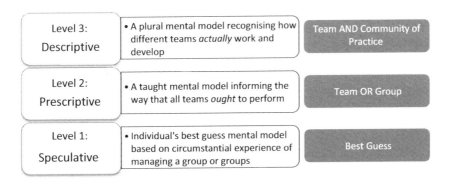

Figure 2.1 The typology of mental models.

To combine the approaches of the two schools, however, both must overcome assumptions which either overemphasise or underemphasise the application of their solution. For the Team School, the assumption is that all managers have the same polarised choice – group or team. For the Community of Practice School, the assumption is that such groups only sit outside the formal structure of organisations.

A new mental model would therefore provide managers with a new choice based on understanding how their direct reports actually operate. They could then select to lead their direct reports as a team or lead them as a community of practice.

Notes

1 Team-related training includes management training, team development and coaching/mentoring training.
2 The term 'training' includes development, learning, coaching, reading, etc. I use the term for convenience. It is not the nature of the training that I am highlighting that is the issue, but the mental model that is projected through it.
3 A small historical comment by Etienne Wenger added during the production of this book: "Even in the early days we never meant to intimate that communities of practice could not or should not have a formal structure in organizations. In fact, there are a number of them. The community of practice I studied for my PhD and ended up being the running example of my 1998 book was an Extra-Dependent Team, all reporting to the same manager. But I do think that our need to contrast communities of practice to teams did mislead some into thinking that way."

References

Allen, N J and Hecht, T D (2004) The 'romance of teams': Toward an understanding of its psychological underpinnings and implications, *Journal of Occupational and Organizational Psychology*, 439–61.

Belbin, M (2004) *Management Teams: Why They Succeed or Fail*, Heinemann, London.

Clutterbuck, D (2007) *Coaching the Team at Work*, Nicholas Brealey, London.

Goffee, R and Jones, G (2006) *Why Should Anyone Be Led by You? What It Takes to Be an Authentic Leader*, Harvard Business School Press, Boston, MA.

Hackman, R and Wageman, R (2001) *Top Teams: Why Some Work and Some Do Not*, Hay Group, Philadelphia, PA.

Harvard Management Update (2008) Why Some Teams Succeed (and so Many Don't), HBR.Org, 28 February, http://blogs.hbr.org/2008/02/why-some-teams-succeed-and-so-1/

Hawkins, P (ed.) (2014) *Leadership Team Coaching in Practice*, Kogan Page, London.

Hughes, J, Jewson, N and Unwin, L (2007) *Communities of Practice: Critical Perspectives*, Routledge, London.

Katzenbach, J and Smith, D (1993) *The Wisdom of Teams: Creating the High-Performance Organization*, Harvard Business School Press, Harvard, MA.

Lave, J and Wenger, E (1991) *Situated Learning: Legitimate Peripheral Participation*, Cambridge University Press, New York.

Lencioni, P (2002) *The Five Dysfunctions of a Team*, Jossey-Bass, San Francisco.

Lord, P and Miller, C (directors) (2014) The Lego Movie.

McChrystal, S, Collins, T, Silverman, D and Fussell, C (2015) *Team of Teams: New Rules of Engagement for a Complex World*, Penguin, New York.

McDermott, R and Archibald, D (2010) Harnessing Your Staff's Informal Networks, *Harvard Business Review*, March.

Myers & Briggs Foundation (2017) MBTI basics, Myers & Briggs Foundation, 18 October, www.myersbriggs.org/my-mbti-personality-type/mbti-basics/home.htm?bhcp=1

National Institute of Adult Continuing Education (2009) *The Private Training Market in the UK*, National Institute of Adult Continuing Education, Leicester.

Revans, R W (1982) *The Origins and Growth of Action Learning*, Chartwell-Bratt, Lund.

Robbins, H and Finley, M (2000) *The new why teams don't work: What goes wrong and how to make it right*, Berrett-Koehler, San Francisco.

Senge, P (1990) *The Fifth Discipline: The Art and Practice of the Learning Organization*, Doubleday/Currency, New York.

Tuckman, B W (1965) Developmental sequence in small groups, *Psychological Bulletin*, 63, 384–99.

Wageman, R, Nunes, D A, Burruss, J A and Hackman, J R (2008) *Senior Leadership Teams*, Harvard Business School Press, Harvard, MA.

Weber, L. (2015). At Work: The Wall Street Journal. *Wall Street Journal*, 2 April, https://blogs.wsj.com/atwork/2015/04/02/what-do-workers-want-from-the-boss/?mod=e2tw

Wenger, E (1998) *Communities of Practice: Learning, Meaning and Identity*, Cambridge University Press, New York.

Wenger, E, McDermott, R and Snyder, W M (2002) *Cultivating Communities of Practice: A Guide to Managing Knowledge*, Harvard Business School Publishing, Boston, MA.

West, M, Armit, K, Loewenthal, L, Eckert, R, West, T and Lee, A (2015). Leadership and Leadership Development in Healthcare: The Evidence Base, King's Fund, February, www.kingsfund.org.uk, www.kingsfund.org.uk/publications/leadership-and-leadership-development-health-care

3 Inter-Dependent and Extra-Dependent Teams

Malinda was a young, athletic, fiery and extremely bright manager heading up a risk management team within a large specialist construction company that covers the whole of the UK.[1] In 2011 the company started to implement a strategy of devolution where decision making once held at a national, centralised level was now to be decentralised to regional levels.

The company had a poor reputation of late delivery and high costs. Good risk management was increasingly seen as a specialist area that would make a difference to the future of the company. Devolution meant that each region's leadership team was responsible for the delivery of construction work – on time and on budget.

As Head of Risk at a national level, Malinda's role was to ensure that risk management was complete and comprehensive across the whole country. This involved ensuring that the right organisational framework, procedures, knowledge, skills and governance were all in place so that, nationally, the biggest risks could be understood and avoided or mitigated.

Malinda had eight direct reports to help her achieve this. Seven were regional risk managers with experience of managing risk in the company, or in other organisations. With risk management devolved to regions, each regional risk manager provided specialist support to help their respective region's leadership team understand the risks that were being run and what options were open to manage them. Such was the specialism of the construction and the number of projects in which each region was involved that each regional risk manager had a team of risk analysts who helped to provide the breadth and depth of support required. The size of the function (approximately 80 staff) meant that the eighth risk manager was responsible for change projects within the function.

Malinda had led teams before. She had been rugby captain at university and had led numerous projects as a consultant in risk management over many years since. She had taken on the job in this company because she saw the importance of the role, knew that it would be difficult and relished the challenge.

When she arrived the nature of the difficulty was all too apparent:

- procedures were imprecise and inconsistent;
- skills within her team with regards to managing risk were variable;

- few people outside of the risk team did any work on managing risk, even though it was within their role description to do so;
- risk analysists would do the risk management on behalf of each project;
- risk analysists weren't finding the time to provide the level of specialist risk management required to get a complete and accurate picture of the risks being run within each region;
- some regions were at breaking point in terms of being able to deliver everything that they had promised within time and budget. Risk management in these regions was similarly at breaking point with people working long hours and experiencing very high levels of stress;
- everyone was complaining of having too much to do;
- one regional risk manager had taken long-term sickness due to stress;
- all regional risk managers wanted more resources;
- the regional risk managers weren't acting as an effective team should.

It was clear to Malinda that something had to change to provide the quality and consistency of risk management required for the company to survive.

One of the main choices that Malinda made early on in her job was to whom the regional risk managers would report. The choice was either to her at a national level or to their regional director. The latter provided the intimacy and flexibility required to keep a close eye on risk and manage it well. But the former offered the stronger governance needed to challenge the regional directors and leadership teams to identify and manage their own risks better. Malinda therefore chose to manage the regional risk managers directly, leaving them to have a 'dotted line' relationship with their regional director (Figure 3.1).

Let's take stock of the situation and explore how the conventional mental model of teams might approach Malinda's challenge.

Approach 1: the conventional mental model of teams

The conventional mental model of teams as reinforced by the Team School would approach the situation with the assumption that all groups can become teams and that teams are the only way to improve performance.

Figure 3.1 Organogram of risk-management team.

Therefore, they would see the problem in the situation straight away: Malinda's direct reports are working in their own individual silos and as a result the whole team is dysfunctional. It's not a team; it's a group. The prescriptive solution would therefore be for Malinda to turn them into a real team. Only then would she achieve the performance upturn required to get everything done and reduce everyone's stress levels. The conventional mental model of teams would ensure that one of the first actions to take would be to clarify the common goal required for everyone to work together to achieve. That common goal would be whatever level of performance the organisation required of the whole team. To ensure that this common goal would be achieved, the team would need to work together. Working together would require Malinda to generate interdependency across the team. The prescriptive approach would ensure Malinda focused on individual strengths within the team, carving out team roles that make the best use of what people are best at. Each direct report would therefore have a unique contribution to the team and together they would be interdependent. Malinda's role in this would be to ensure the team worked together. By holding regular meetings with the team, she could ensure they made solid decisions, coordinated activity and monitored progress towards the common goal. As a result, the team would deliver what the organisation wanted of them and the pressure and stress that they were feeling would be reduced.

Approach 2: the plural mental model of teams

Using the plural mental model of teams, Malinda has two different ways of understanding what is going on with her team and therefore two different options to pursue based on that assessment. It is easy to recognise that each regional risk manager shares the same practice – they do the same job and require similar levels of skill and knowledge to do that job. Malinda doesn't need to conclude that the regional risk managers are dysfunctional just because they focus on their own respective regions and don't work together. Instead, she can stop worrying in the knowledge that such individual behaviour is entirely functional. Having stopped adding to her own stress levels, Malinda's attention can be on observing and facilitating how the team learns from each other's individual experiences when doing the same work, so that they can develop greater consistency of practice across the team. Malinda's leadership role is therefore about enabling the sharing of practice amongst the team by holding regular team meetings for exactly that purpose. At these meetings, regional risk managers can share their individual challenges to get ideas from their peers, learn from the successes of others and from the mistakes that their colleagues have made.

With a plural mental model, Malinda would know that each direct report needed to be held individually accountable for their respective region, rather than collectively and mutually accountable for all regions. She would, however, ensure that each regional risk manager was developing the full repertoire of skills required to support their region. The team meetings would therefore become particularly valuable to everyone as some people would be better at some things than others. But through sharing the learning at such meetings, everyone would have the opportunity to improve their ability to perform in their individual region. As this learning process was collective, the whole team's combined performance would also increase. As a result, the team would deliver what the organisation wanted of them and the pressure and stress that they were feeling would be reduced.

Personal reflection

As you read through these two approaches, what thoughts do you notice you have? What personal experiences are you tapping into as you try to relate to Malinda's situation? If you were Malinda, what would you do? Are you noticing a favouritism towards one approach over another? What is the source of the influence of that favouritism?

You may have noticed that the final sentence in each approach is identical. That is because both schools of thought offer performance improvement – not just in raw numbers, but also in people's engagement in the team and its value to the wider organisation. But which is right? Convention would have us maintain that the Team School is the only option. But the Community of Practice School, when applied in this context, becomes a viable alternative. Indeed, it is my contention that the Community of Practice School of thinking is better applied to teams like Malinda's – teams where members all have similar roles and skills and who work principally with people outside of the team rather than inside the team. This contention does not dismiss the importance of the Team School, but it does provide a clearer context to the application of the Team School's thinking: not all teams will benefit from trying to turn it into an Inter-Dependent Team; some teams will benefit from being treated as if it were a community of practice.

But which approach does a manager take with their team? The determining factor should not be the favouritism of the manager, but the nature of the team itself. Where team members all have different roles and skills, the Team School approach is valid. Where team members all have similar roles and skills, the Community of Practice School approach is valid. This is the nature of the plural mental model for teams. But before we explore what this looks like in practice, we need to change the clumsy nature of the language being used.

A new vocabulary

In Chapter 2 – Schools of herding – we briefly discussed that the dominance of the Team School had led to all direct reports collectively being referred to as a 'team' – irrespective of whether they were or not. Historically, direct reports might have been called a gang, party, band, shift, squad or crew. But these have all since been superseded by the word 'team'. Thus, the language of 'group versus team' has shifted to 'effective versus ineffective team'. The word 'team' is therefore pre-eminent.

This pre-eminence of the language of 'team' has been further amplified by encultured beliefs held by line managers about leadership. The logic of these beliefs goes: good managers are seen as leaders; leaders lead teams; I have direct reports; therefore, for me to be a leader my direct reports must constitute a team. Aspirational managers therefore typically consider they lead a team. For the work of communities of practice to become an accessible alternative to the work of the Team School, a new vocabulary needs to be developed. Since 'team' is so pre-eminent, the word 'team' needs to be used. But the two types of 'team' still need to be distinguished. To do that I have focused on the nature of dependency that each team has. The new language of the plural mental model of teams is therefore of Inter-Dependent Teams and Extra-Dependent Teams.[2] Let's now look at how dependency and other factors affect their distinction.

Inter-Dependent Teams and Extra-Dependent Teams

Inter-Dependent Teams most resemble the effective team as espoused by the Team School. Team members have complementary skills and depend on each other to achieve. In a formal organisational structure, they are defined as a managed group of people who all *work* together to *achieve* a common *goal*. Extra-Dependent Teams most resemble a community of practice as espoused by the Community of Practice School. Team members all have similar roles and skills and use them with people outside the team – hence the word *extra* in the name. In a formal organisational structure they are defined as a managed group of people *learning* together to *develop* a common *practice*.

The plural mental model of teams recognises and accepts that both types of team are legitimate within organisations. Indeed, later in this chapter I explain how, even though the plural mental model is new, Extra-Dependent Teams are easy to find in most organisations. That is because Extra-Dependent Teams complement Inter-Dependent Teams in organisations. This will be explored later in the chapter, but for now, let's explore the differences in Table 3.1.

Different versus similar skills

The most noticeable distinction between the two types of team is that Inter-Dependent Teams are made up of people with *different* roles and skills, whilst Extra-Dependent Teams are made up of people with *similar* roles and skills. For instance, in Malinda's team earlier in this chapter, all the team

Table 3.1 Inter-Dependent and Extra-Dependent Team distinctions

Inter-Dependent Teams	Extra-Dependent Teams
• *Definition* – 'Working together to achieve a common goal'.	• *Definition* – 'Learning together to develop a common practice'.
• *Inter*-dependent – people depend on each other in the team to perform.	• *Extra-dependent* – team members depend on other people outside the team to perform.
• *Different skills* – people who work together *because* their different skills are required to achieve the goal.	• *Similar skills* – people who learn together *because* they have similar skills and do similar work.
• *Common goal* – everyone has the same, singular, unifying goal to achieve.	• *Common practice* – everyone working in similar ways, using similar equipment and similar standards but on different work.
• *Mutual accountability* – Inter-dependence ensures there is mutual accountability for achieving the common goal.	• *Individual accountability* – Extra-dependence ensures individual accountability for achieving comparable goals.
• *Improving combined performance* – through working together better.	• *Improving combined performance* – through learning better together.

members were regional risk managers. With the same role, they required similar skills in identifying, analysing and managing risk in their region. Not only that, but they followed similar processes, used similar equipment and used similar language. A key test of similarity is the ability to move positions within a team with minimum effort. For instance, in Malinda's team it would be easy for the regional risk manager for the north to move to become the regional risk manager for the south because, even though the region is different, the skills and knowledge used are much the same. That's not to say that such skills, processes, equipment or language need to be *identical*. But where similarity exists within an Extra-Dependent Team there is a need to generate greater similarity to provide the consistency required for combined performance. For instance, Malinda's team had ongoing debates about which software to use for what risk analysis and what was the precise name to call such risk analysis. The team was naturally inclined towards establishing greater similarity in their repertoire of skills.

Contrast that with an Inter-Dependent Team such as the regional director's team that the regional risk manager supports. Such a team is made up of a regional director and heads of delivery, programme control, engineering, human resources, safety, finance and commercial (see Figure 3.2). Each member of the team brings a different set of skills and knowledge to the team. This difference can be tested by the ability of one team member to do the job of another team member; the head of engineering, for instance, would not be expected to be able to do the job of head of finance, and vice versa. Each team member has a unique repertoire of skills and knowledge to bring to the team. Difference is the key to success

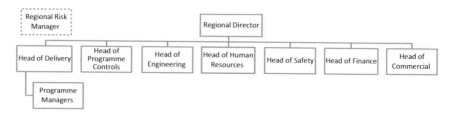

Figure 3.2 Organogram of regional Inter-Dependent Teams.

in Inter-Dependent Teams whilst similarity is the key to success in Extra-Dependent Teams.

Inter- versus extra-dependency

The nature of dependency is easily understood through understanding the impact of losing what you depend on. When you depend on someone, losing them means that you can't do what you can only do together. Consider a mother and father. Both depend on each other to conceive naturally. Without one of them, it doesn't matter which, a naturally conceived baby is not possible. To team together for a baby, they therefore depend on each other – they are inter-dependent.

Compare the mother and father example with an antenatal class of prospective first-time mothers and fathers. Do they depend on each other to prepare for childbirth? We can test this dependency by losing some of them and understanding the impact. If half of the couples failed to turn up to a class, the actual impact would probably be that the class would continue as normal. The couples therefore don't depend on each other. Acknowledging this non-dependency is at the heart of understanding extra-dependency. Because when it comes to the work of childbirth, each couple will depend on the midwife being in attendance – they don't need the other couples from the antenatal class. The probability of the birth being smooth and safe is increased by the addition of other experts on hand such as a paediatrician and an anaesthetist. For the antenatal class therefore, extra-dependency means not depending on each other in the class but depending on people outside of the class.

Apply that idea to Malinda's team. Her regional risk managers don't depend on each other to succeed in their own regions. One could fail to achieve in a particular region and it would not have any impact on any of the other regions. Each regional risk manager could still perform. But that performance is dependent on people within their region playing their part, such as programme managers identifying and recording risks accurately. Without that a regional risk manager could not be entirely successful in their role. Reciprocally, programme managers depend on regional risk managers to provide analysis and guidance on how to manage that risk. The relationship between regional risk managers *inside* Malinda's team is therefore extra-dependent, whilst each regional risk manager's relationship with certain people like the programme managers *outside* the team is inter-dependent.

At this point it is worth distinguishing the difference between dependency and benefit. Dependency requires need: a regional risk manager and programme manager need each other so that they can both be successful. Their dependence on each other is mutual. Benefit on the other hand is about achieving advantage. Whilst regional risk managers are not mutually dependent, they do mutually benefit from sharing and learning from each other's experiences and knowledge. So whilst the team of regional risk managers don't have mutual *dependence*, there remains huge potential for *mutual benefit*. For instance, should a regional risk manager learn how to persuade a programme manager to identify risks more accurately, then sharing this learning with others in the team is beneficial to them.

Common goal versus common practice

Critical to understanding Inter-Dependent and Extra-Dependent Teams is realising what bonds them. For an Inter-Dependent Team, the bond is the common goal. Teams that have a need for each other only have that need when there is a common goal to achieve together. That is why the Team School makes so much of the need for a common goal. For members of an Extra-Dependent Team, on the other hand, the bond is their common practice. The common practice involves skills, processes, equipment, language and other aspects. The common practice is also likely to involve having similar standards of performance, similar key performance indicators and even identical goals.

Having *identical* goals and having a common goal are fundamentally different. The goal of a prospective mother and father is to have a baby. This is a single goal, common to them both. By contrast, all the couples in the antenatal class have an identical goal – to have a baby. But that does not make them have a common, shared, single, unifying goal. Common goals are the domain of the Inter-Dependent Team. Teams that fail are often cited by the Team School as not having a clear enough common goal. For Katzenbach and Smith the common goal is a *team work-product* that is the summation of individual job objectives. They say, 'to be effective, team work-products must require roughly equivalent contributions from all the people on the team to make something specific happen' (Katzenbach and Smith, 1993). The team is therefore combining to achieve a common goal that only its members' equal and necessary contributions can achieve for the organisation.

But this attempt at being specific about defining a common goal remains paradoxically woolly. In the English language (http://dictionary.com, 2017), the word common can mean two very different things:

1   belonging equally to (as in a common land or property);
2   frequent occurrence (as in a common mistake).

The same issue arises with the word 'shared' which I have heard as a way of trying to clarify what is meant by the term common. But sharing the same *genes* in your body as an identical twin and sharing the same *jeans* with an identical twin are completely different ways of using the word sharing. The same is the case with the word 'common'. A common goal that belongs equally to everyone in the team is therefore a singular goal that unifies everyone's output. This is the common goal that is required of an Inter-Dependent Team and the common goal that Katzenbach and Smith are trying to explain above. However, I have witnessed managers and team members of Extra-Dependent Teams convince themselves that they constitute the conventional mental model of teams because they have a 'common goal' that frequently occurs across the team. The Team School is not espousing this second definition of 'common' as it doesn't require interdependency.

The frequent occurrence definition of common does, however, match the similarities required of the Community of Practice School. A common practice involves all members having similar standards and using similar techniques as each other. This therefore might include achieving an identical goal in terms of output or performance. For the purposes of clarity as you continue to read this book, I will describe goals for Extra-Dependent Teams as comparable and a goal for Inter-Dependent Teams as common.

Mutual versus individual accountability

In Inter-Dependent Teams mutual accountability is essential for success because, without it, team members don't have commitment to the common goal. Team sports are the easiest examples of mutual accountability in teams. In a rugby team everyone is working towards a common goal – winning the match by scoring at least one more point than the opposition. Whilst different members of the team have different skills and roles, one will be the team member who scores the points that take them beyond the opposition's score at the final whistle. Mutual accountability recognises that everyone has contributed to the win, not just the person who scored the final points. Similarly, should the team lose, mutual accountability acknowledges that everyone is accountable for the loss. Teams that make too much of a star player or seek to blame an individual for losing a match generate dysfunction and fail to perform.

By contrast, an Extra-Dependent Team has individual accountability because each member has a comparable, individual goal. Mutual accountability is difficult to achieve where everyone is doing the same role, with the same skills but each delivering to different people (read more on this in Chapter 7). This is important to acknowledge because the people who depend on that individual are outside the team. The goal is therefore achieved by that individual without the direct involvement of anyone else inside the Extra-Dependent Team. Whilst the conventional mental model of teams would have us insist on mutual accountability across the whole team for performance goals, the reality is that goals are individual. This individuality matches the non-dependency between Extra-Dependent Team members. This is one of the fundamental factors behind understanding why Extra-Dependent Teams can be like 'herding cats'.

For instance, one of Malinda's team, Valerie, had been working hard to get more resources from her regional director. After several proposals, presentations and meetings, the agreement was made providing her with an enhanced team of risk analysts with which to provide better-quality risk management support. Such a result provided the means for that regional risk manager to achieve her individual goal. No one else worked with Valerie to help her achieve, so no one else could claim to be mutually accountable for that outcome. Instead, Valerie had individual accountability.

Of course, the same is also true when things go bad. For instance, another regional risk manager, Tony, was an experienced risk manager and had a background in leading teams. When he joined Malinda's team his allocated region was already struggling to deliver. After joining the team things just seemed to get worse with costs and deadlines spiralling out of control. But few of the other regional risk managers came to Tony's aid. Whilst within an Inter-Dependent Team this would be seen as dysfunctional behaviour, within an Extra-Dependent Team this is to be expected because the other regional risk managers each had other regions depending on them. Therefore, if they were to support Tony instead, they might jeopardise the performance of their own region.

But before thinking that individual responsibility within an Extra-Dependent Team means being selfish and non-collaborative, the opposite is the case – just not in the way that the conventional team mental model would have us believe. Tony's *mutual* accountability was to his region. Because he was dependent on programme managers and they were dependent on him, mutual accountability was needed in how they achieved together within the region. So, if the region was unsuccessful, then so was Tony. And if Tony was unsuccessful, so was the region.

Extra-Dependent Teams therefore have *individual* accountability *within* the team, but they require *mutual* accountability with others *outside* the team. Because of this, Extra-Dependent Teams provide a vital function within organisations in that they provide a complementary connection between teams within organisations. In effect, they are the glue within the organisational matrix. Rather than being inwardly focused with mutual accountability on their own common goal as Inter-Dependent Teams need to be, their function is to provide outwardly focused expertise interdependently with others outside the team. Extra-Dependent Team members really need to be conventional team players, but more to those *outside* the team than inside it. For those inside the team, they need to be co-learners, a very different type of collaboration.

Working together better versus learning better together

Even though there are clear distinctions between Inter-Dependent and Extra-Dependent Teams, both are equally able to improve the combined performance of the team. For an Inter-Dependent Team, improvement is through *working together better*. There are two important parts to this phrase. Firstly, working together. People in Inter-Dependent Teams apply their existing capability in combination with different capability from other team members to achieve their mutually accountable common goal. To get better at this, the team might concentrate on fine-tuning roles, addressing communications between members, getting more precise in their decision making or ensuring that everyone is indeed working towards the same unifying goal. As a result, the Inter-Dependent Team works together, better.

By contrast, Extra-Dependent Teams *learn better together*. Again, there are two parts to this phrase. Firstly, learning better. Learning is the act of improving skills, knowledge and capabilities. The only way that an Extra-Dependent Team can improve is if each member learns, because the repertoire of skills and knowledge that each member has is the limit of each member's ability to perform. Critically, the slower the member of the Extra-Dependent Team learns, the less able they are to improve their performance. Learning better therefore is about the speed at which individuals learn their practice. As we will see in subsequent chapters, learning is not simply about what is taught; it also includes how an individual learns on the job and how fast they learn. For instance, how they conduct experiments with different ways of doing things rather than simply pointing out that things are inadequate, or the depth at which they reflect on mistakes so that they can ensure they are successful next time, or even how they pay attention to what has made them successful and reinforce this skill and knowledge. All these sorts of activities will enable a member of an Extra-Dependent Team to improve.

The second part of the phrase is *together*. As we discussed above, Extra-Dependent Teams have the potential to gain huge benefit from each other because of their unique common practice – the people who most experience what they experience at work are in their team. So where one person learns from an experiment, another learns from a mistake, and a third learns from being successful. All members of the same Extra-Dependent Team can learn from each other, faster – so long as they learn together.

Locating Extra-Dependent Teams in organisations

Once someone is introduced to the distinction between Inter-Dependent Teams and Extra-Dependent Teams they are relatively easy to identify in organisations. For instance, when I run a workshop on Extra-Dependent Teams I ask managers to map the part of the organisation they work in. Afterwards, I ask them to identify which line-managed teams are structured as Inter-Dependent Teams and which are structured as Extra-Dependent

Teams. Managers easily identify both Inter-Dependent and Extra-Dependent Teams within their organisation. Given the dominance of the Team School and the conventional mental model of teams, it might be thought that Inter-Dependent Teams made up the vast majority of teams in organisations and that Extra-Dependent Teams were uncommon. Actually, Extra-Dependent Teams are common, even as common as Inter-Dependent Teams.

I conducted some research with a number of managers by way of follow-up to the Extra-Dependent Team workshops they had attended. I asked them to access an official organisational diagram for the part of their organisation that they were most familiar with. Organisational diagrams capture the line-management responsibility which is what I wanted to identify.

Working systematically through the formal structure presented on the organisational chart, I asked each person to determine the line responsibility of each manager's direct reports. I gave them four options to choose from: either they identified the line manager's team to be Inter-Dependent, Extra-Dependent, a mixture of both or, if they didn't know the team well enough, the last option was to decide it was unknown. Where a team was determined Inter-Dependent, it was clear from the organisational structure and the person's knowledge of the team that 80 per cent of the team had different roles. Where a team was determined as Extra-Dependent, this was in favour of 80 per cent or more having similar job roles. The mixed teams were teams made up of a mix of similar and different roles where neither was more than 80 per cent.

Three examples of the results are shown in Figure 3.3. The results presented here are from completely different organisations showing evidence that a wide variety of organisations have high percentages of Extra-Dependent Teams in them. One is a global private-sector company providing cutting-edge IT software products, another is a UK public-sector organisation providing labour-intensive correction and rehabilitation to ex-prisoners, whilst the third is a business unit within a division of a global pharmaceutical company.

The striking thing about the results is that Extra-Dependent Teams are clearly being designed into large proportions of vastly different organisations. Such findings seem ludicrous – that such distinct groups should be hidden in plain sight within organisations. Of course, this doesn't represent all organisations in all the world. But where people start to recognise the presence of Extra-Dependent Teams, they start to realise they are commonplace. For instance, the person I worked with in the pharmaceutical company indicated that whilst his area was 43 per cent Extra-Dependent Teams, the same structure was used in another two sister business units. These business units were then matched in staff numbers by support functions that the person identified as being made up mostly of Extra-Dependent Teams. All these units constituted a division, one of several divisions that were identified as all very similar within the global company. The person concluded that the proportion of Extra-Dependent Teams in his organisation, made up of some 93,000 staff, was about 50 per cent. It is clear that Extra-Dependent Teams are commonplace.

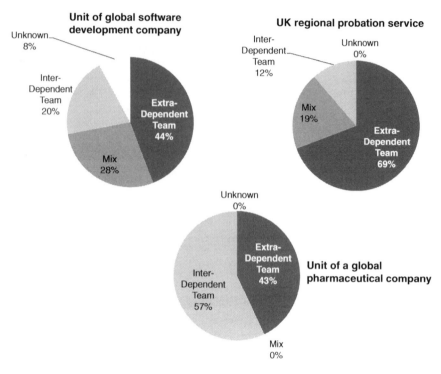

Figure 3.3 Distribution of Inter-Dependent and Extra-Dependent Teams in three different organisations.

Teams that complement each other in organisations

Having a similar proportion of Inter-Dependent and Extra-Dependent Teams in an organisation actually makes a great deal of sense because they have the ability to complement each other. Extra-Dependent Teams provide specialist members to Inter-Dependent Teams who then work together to deliver a common goal.

Compare this with matrix organisations where the conventional mental model of team presides. For a team member with a dotted line to one manager and a solid line to another manager there is 'confusion over who is the boss' (Sy and D'Annunzio, 2005). Having multiple managers to report to, such as within most complex, matrix organisations is an area that the Team School doesn't sufficiently address. If every person is expected to be a member of multiple teams to reflect those multiple reporting managers, there are many questions that line reports are left to answer for themselves (Table 3.2).

The complementary nature of the distinction between teams and communities of practice is identified by Wenger. He says, 'it is often useful to belong to both types at once in order to achieve the synergy of the two forms of

Table 3.2 Confusion in the matrix

Question	Possible answers
Of the two teams, which common goal is the priority?	The manager that shouts the loudest / the goal I think is more important to me / the one with the nicest manager / etc.
How do I deal with issues in one team that directly affect the other team?	I'll complain to one team about the other – and vice versa.
If I pull my weight in one team what happens if I'm not seen to pull my weight in the other?	I'll do just enough to get the balance between the two.
What happens if the respective managers don't communicate with each other?	That's OK, I can play one off against the other.
Who do I turn to if I have an issue?	I'll turn to the one who's most likely to give me the help I want. If I don't get what I want, I'll turn to the other one.
Who really knows what I do?	And do they really care?

engagement. For example, a specialist on a team made up of complementary competences will usually benefit from also belonging to a community of practice of peers who share their specialization' (Wenger, 1998, p. 76). Wenger is talking directly to what complements Inter-Dependent and Extra-Dependent Teams. Extra-Dependent Teams in organisations there-fore enable organisations to connect better together, to work compatibly and to perform in alignment. More of this is covered in Chapter 7, Extra-Dependent Team performance.

With Extra-Dependent Teams providing an important compatibility to the organisational matrix, and with them being easy to identify, it's interest-ing to understand what makes people blind to them.

What stops people seeing Extra-Dependent Teams?

Above all else, the one factor that stops people seeing Extra-Dependent Teams is their devotion to the Team School and the conventional mental model of teams. But there are several specific factors that I have identified that blind people to Extra-Dependent Teams, as follows.

Sibling rivalry

This first factor is analogous to sibling rivalry. I was brought up as one of four siblings. We got on fine, but if anyone outside the family suggested that any of us looked like one of the others, it really got our backs up! Whilst everyone on the outside of the family could see clear similarities with all four siblings, the sibling rivalry on the inside meant that we focused entirely on the differences between us. This factor also happens in Extra-Dependent

Teams. For instance, I worked with a team of matrons who all did similar work, with essentially the same role and skills, albeit in a different health-care group within a hospital. Many key stakeholders to the matrons saw them as all the same – for good or bad. Even the hospital regulator, the Care Quality Commission, reported on the matrons as if they were a group based on similarity. However, when talking to the matrons themselves, they per-sistently distinguished themselves from each other. They couldn't see what those outside the team could see.

Specialised differences

This factor builds on sibling rivalry in that members within an Extra-Dependent Team will tend to consider themselves different because of their specialisms in the particular common practice. For instance, I worked with a head of engineering who had a team of seven engineers, all of whom sup-ported different construction projects. Because each engineer had a particu-lar engineering specialism, he saw each as distinctly different and treated them as if they were an Inter-Dependent Team. In fact, whilst each engineer assumed their speciality within each project, all the engineering specialisms were required to a lesser extent. Engineers therefore really needed to be more skilful and knowledgeable about all the other engineering specialisms to best support their projects. The manager eventually started to see and then develop the similarity in the team.

Prejudice

I worked with a group of different managers in a hospital. Following an explanation of the difference between Inter-Dependent and Extra-Dependent Teams I ran two exercises one after the other. Firstly, in pairs, I got them to explore a scenario of a building company and asked them to identify where in the organisation they recognised Inter-Dependent and Extra-Dependent Teams. They easily found them, and these matched my own analysis. What none of them knew was that I had built that sce-nario with one of their colleagues prior to the event and based it around their own hospital situation. Any reference to builders, plumbers and site managers was entirely invented to replace references to nurses, doctors and ward managers. The second exercise was therefore almost identical to the first, but with the organisation's name and the job titles changed. The reaction by the hospital managers to the second exercise was fascinat-ing. Firstly, they didn't recognise the similarity in the scenarios; to them they were completely different. Secondly, they determined that some of the teams they had identified as extra-dependent in the first exercise were identified in the second exercise as inter-dependent. Whilst they could see Extra-Dependent Teams in other organisations, they found it difficult to see them in their own organisation and found it particularly difficult to see Extra-Dependent Teams when that team was like their own. When it came to their own teams, they had a prejudice for seeing themselves as inter-dependent.

Scientifically identified differences

Profiling of teams for differences is ubiquitous and rarely questioned. Two types of profiles are popular for identifying difference: personality and behaviour. Whilst such differences are both interesting and useful at times, the fact that personality or behavioural differences exist between people does no more to bond an Inter-Dependent Team together as it would create a team out of two random people who just happened to be different. But personality and behavioural profiling tools are commonly used to identify difference and, as a result, people are biased towards Inter-Dependent Teams, even if they are in an Extra-Dependent Team.

Two such techniques, one personality, the other behavioural, are commonly practised by consultants inside and outside organisations. The first is the Myers-Briggs Type Indicator which differentiates personality type using four different measures. The essence of the theory behind the tool is that 'much seemingly random variation in [people's] behavior is actually quite orderly and consistent, being due to basic differences' (Myers & Briggs Foundation, 2017). It is an ubiquitous tool which is frequently used with groups, and is cited as a tool for team development due to its scientific validity in highlighting differences within a team (Lencioni, 2002). Highlighting the scientific validity of such difference can lead people in Extra-Dependent Teams to consider such difference to justify their compliance with the conventional mental model of team when in fact they would be better acknowledging their similarities and developing their team fundamentally differently.

The second model of teams is Meredith Belbin's team roles. As Belbin's own website advocates, 'wherever teams exist within organisations, Belbin can be used to bring the right people together so that the team is as high performing as possible, and is more likely to achieve its goals' (Belbin, 2017). It professes to identify strengths and weaknesses in defined behaviours associated with working in a team. The idea is that having a balance of these behaviours across all members will enable the team to become high performing. Belbin originally identified these team roles from observing participants on a ten-week course for successful managers with board-level potential. One element of the course involved participants working in competing teams on a week-long business simulation. He identified that the most successful teams were not the most intellectual, but the most balanced in terms of certain team behaviours – he calls them the nine Belbin team roles. Users of the Belbin team roles will find it difficult to acknowledge Extra-Dependent Teams because of two assumptions made in Belbin's research. Firstly, it assumes all teams work together. This reinforces its alignment to Inter-Dependent Teams. Secondly, and rather ironically, the cohort of participants technically constituted a community of practice – they were similar in that they were all aspiring executives *learning* together. Given their similarity, when they were required to *work* together to achieve a common goal on the business simulation, they would need to find differences between them to succeed. Given the lack of any other opportunities to be different within a simulation (for instance, experience in post, experience of a role, knowledge of the work, relationship with clients, etc.), it is no wonder that behaviour difference between team members become the defining success criteria. For our purposes here, it highlights the *requirement* of the Team School to find difference in groups of people, even when similarity is so pronounced. As a result, 'scientific' approaches to identifying differences become blind to the existence of Extra-Dependent Teams – even when they are in front of their very eyes.

Layers of difference

Another way that people see difference in Extra-Dependent Teams is when there are layers of experience within a team. For instance, I worked with a team in a bank who dealt with risks and incidents of financial crime, mainly money laundering. The team was made up of six senior members, each of whom operated in a different territory supported by a deputy. The deputy was typically less experienced than the senior in each. The range of territories coupled with the different levels in experience made many see differences. Extra-Dependent Teams recognise layers of inexperience within a team but acknowledge that such difference is people's different waypoints on a similar learning journey. These layers are very important to acknowledge in an Extra-Dependent Team and Chapter 5, Extra-Dependent Team dynamics, comprehensively explores this point.

Mixed teams

In the research into different organisations' formal structures, it was identified that some teams are a mixture of inter-dependent and extra-dependent members. Because of this mix the conventional mental model of teams dominates since there is strong evidence of difference and dependencies between team members. But dysfunctionality is typically present. For instance, I worked with a reward team in a bank. Many of the team members were heads of reward in different divisions within the bank, but some had unique roles such as the operations officer, the head of pensions and the head of group compensation. The manager of the team was clear that dysfunction wasn't with these areas of difference, but with the divisional 'heads of' – who did the same roles. Clearly, the team was made up of a mix of Inter-Dependent and Extra-Dependent Teams. The manager surrounded herself with the unique roles and worked easily with them, but couldn't understand why those with the similar divisional roles didn't work like a team. This small group of Inter-Dependent Team members were blind to the different needs of the Extra-Dependent Team members.

Manager dependency

A very important reason why people find it difficult to see or acknowledge Extra-Dependent Teams is because the only person who does depend on everyone in the team is the manager. As we have already discussed, the individual goals of Extra-Dependent Team members mean that members are not mutually accountable within the team. However, one person really feels the pressure of this – the manager. Managers of Extra-Dependent Teams are accountable for the total performance of all their team members. Therefore they, and they alone, are dependent on the performance of each and every team member. This is the reason why managers cling to the idea that their team is inter-dependent – because it is in their self-interest for everyone in the team to help them achieve the performance goal they are responsible for achieving. The conventional mental model of teams is highly appealing to the line manager – everyone working together to achieve a common goal – because it also happens to be their goal!

When my own mental model matched the conventional model of teams, many years ago, I would facilitate team-development workshops in direct support of many managers who I now see as managers of Extra-Dependent Teams, yet everything we did on the workshop tried to develop the team towards greater inter-dependency. We focused on setting a common goal (inter-dependency), how the team would work together (inter-dependency) and what personality/behavioural/competence differences might explain issues within the team (inter-dependency). I realise in hindsight that many managers had procured my services because they were blind to the realities of their team and wanted me to provide the team solution as, above everyone else in the team, it favoured them. On reflection I realise that I was perpetuating their situation rather than addressing it.

Ambidextrous organisations

As you read this book you may think that I am making too much of the differences between Inter-Dependent and Extra-Dependent Teams. But I like to think of them as hands. If you focus on your hands, you notice the fingers, the opposable thumb, where they meet the palm and how it joins to the wrist. At this level it is generic and doesn't specify left from right. But the rise of the Team School has been, if we continue the analogy, a bit like researching right-handedness, and then applying that research to both left hands and right hands. Fifty per cent of the time the research will be correct and useful, but for the rest, whilst it looks similar, the application is so much harder to achieve. Indeed, for some it is near impossible to achieve. Yet all the time there is an overwhelming favouritism to right hands and a complete denial to accept that left hands are different.

My argument in this book is that organisations need to be ambidextrous – confident and fluent in their use of both Inter-Dependent and Extra-Dependent Teams. Both teams may look similar, but they have important differences that make them complementary. Only by acknowledging these differences between the two types of teams can their full potential be realised. Only then can the dominance of the 'right-handed' conventional mental model of teams that is supposed to work equally for 'left-handed' teams be replaced by the plural model of teams that allows organisations to realise the power of both 'hands' – Inter-Dependent *and* Extra-Dependent Teams.

Notes

1 The company and team are real but have been anonymised.
2 The evolution of this terminology can be read about in Chapter 10 – Reflection on practice. These terms are not perfect, but they are the ones I have chosen to settle with.

References

Belbin, M (2017). Belbin for teams, Belbin, 18 October, www.belbin.com/belbin-for-teams/

Katzenbach, J and Smith, D (1993) The discipline of teams, *Harvard Business Review*, March–April, 111–20.

Lencioni, P (2002) *The Five Dysfunctions of a Team*, Jossey-Bass, San Francisco.

Myers & Briggs Foundation (2017) MBTI basics, Myers & Briggs Foundation, 18 October, www.myersbriggs.org/my-mbti-personality-type/mbti-basics/home.htm?bhcp=1

Sy, T and D'Annunzio, L (2005). Challenges and strategies of matrix organizations: Top-level and mid-level managers' perspectives, *Human Resource Planning*, March, 39–49.

Wenger, E (1998) *Communities of Practice: Learning, Meaning and Identity*, Cambridge University Press, New York.

Part II

4   The bonding power of Extra-Dependent Teams

Extra-Dependent Teams have a dilemma. On the one hand we have explored the distinctions between Inter-Dependent and Extra-Dependent Teams and also discovered that they are prevalent in organisations. Indeed, we have seen how Inter-Dependent and Extra-Dependent Teams are complementary within a complex matrix organisation. But on the other hand we have also found that the dominance of the Team School and the conventional mental model of teams coupled with other factors highlighted in Chapter 3 mean that Extra-Dependent Teams are difficult to 'see' in organisations – indeed, they aren't even consciously designed into organisations. How come they exist at all? How can something that isn't otherwise acknowledged and can be so difficult to manage occur at all within organisations? The simple answer is that they have a very powerful bond which pulls the team together, irrespective of how it is line managed or which mental model is applied to it. Not only is this bond powerful enough to occur when it is not acknowledged, but where it is acknowledged it is possible to utilise the bond to achieve synergy in a team – more than the sum of the parts. But if this bond is not handled well, ignored or fought against, it can easily become a source of dysfunction. This powerful bond is identity.

Identity

Identity has always been a key aspect of understanding teams. From defining 'the reds' versus 'the blues' in sports teams to giving names to teams – 'the customer service team', 'the transformation team' or 'the board' – all indicate the power of identity to draw people together.

In the last few decades some particularly astute research has been conducted by academics working with Social Identity Theory (Haslam et al., 2003, 2011). In this work what particularly resonates with understanding teams is the notion of identity being determined collectively rather than individually – the notion of 'we-ness' rather than 'me-ness'. In essence, the idea has a number of important aspects which help us to understand the power of Extra-Dependent Teams.

Firstly, identity is a psychological process that requires social interaction. I can only know who I am through comparing myself with others. I might think of others as more or less similar to me and I might think of me as more or less different to them. Such a process is called 'self-categorisation'. At its simplest level it means someone might self-categorise as a woman because they are more similar to a woman than a man. By way of enhancing their categorisation as a woman they also make clear distinctions compared to being a man. For instance, they might make distinctions in the way they walk or talk as a woman, as compared to the way men walk or talk. Self-categorisation therefore involves seeking out similarities between members identified as the in-group and distinctions with those seen as the out-group.

This leads to a second element of social identity which involves members of the in-group viewing themselves more favourably compared to outgroups along the dimensions that they value. For a woman this might mean (but is by no means a given) considering herself kinder than men or being smarter than men. It doesn't matter what the basis of the evidence for this is, the in-group will make sense of their identity and accentuate elements that the in-group deem more important to themselves. For instance, if a particular man was found to be smarter and kinder than women, then women might see that man as an 'anomaly', 'a particular case' or even 'not normal'. In this way, it allows the woman to maintain her self-categorisation as a woman – distinct from men (in general, rather than this particular man) and still along the lines favourable to her as a woman.

A third feature of self-categorisation therefore is that it depends on the context. To see oneself within a particular category requires comparative fit *between* the in-group and out-group relative to the wider context. A woman may be likely to identify more strongly as a woman if they are in a distinct minority to men, whilst when identifying themselves within a context of other women they may identify with a different category, such as being a solicitor rather than being a barrister. In both contexts someone may be both a solicitor and a woman, but their self-categorisation may alter because of the context that they are in.

Partnered with this comparative fit is the notion of normative fit – that those *within* a particular in-group talk and act in a way we might expect. So women might get a stronger sense of identity with other women if they dress in the clothes expected of a woman. Similarly, men might reassure their identity as a man if they dress as a man might be expected to dress.

A fifth element of self-categorisation draws again from this normative fit in that as we identify with a particular in-group we start to become more like the norms we associated with the fit. This is called *self-stereotyping*. Believe it or not, we select characteristics of the in-group that we believe represent what it is to be in that in-group and then amplify those characteristics. So men who identify 'man-ness' to involve watching sport, eating heartily and telling jokes actually do *more* of that in order to reinforce their identity as a 'man'. Of course, such things are partly subjectively defined by an individual, but they are also culturally defined as well. For instance, the separation of men and women into separate categories has happened for as long as we can

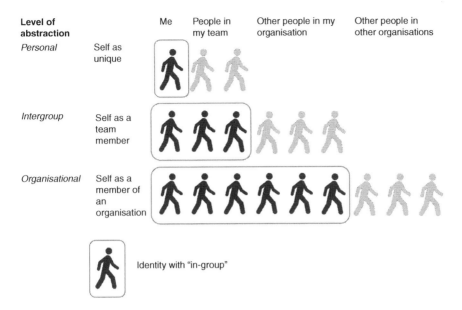

Figure 4.1 Levels of abstraction.

know. Such separation is then reinforced through the way we structure our environment and the language we use. When we use a public toilet, for example, we are required to choose whether we identify as a man or a woman. Laws regarding the use of public toilets then ensure that such a choice isn't necessarily ours to make alone. Walking into the 'wrong' toilet may well generate an unpleasant reaction from another user who, rather than welcoming you as an in-group member, identifies you as very much a member of the out-group.

Of course, men and women, along with anyone identifying as neither gender or both, are all people. This leads to a final point about self-categorising in that we abstract up or down to generate more or less inclusivity. Such changes in categorisation is referred to as *levels of abstraction*. Describing everyone as 'people' includes all genders and so is abstracting up a level from describing everyone as either men or women. As a member of a team in an organisation, you might use different levels of abstraction to self-categorise for different contexts, as highlighted in Figure 4.1.

Identity in Extra-Dependent Teams

How does this relate to Extra-Dependent Teams? Extra-Dependent Teams are made up of people with similarities – they do similar work, have similar roles, have similar skills, use similar processes, use similar equipment, indeed they may even have similar careers. This similarity helps create a sense of 'we-ness' within the team. Understanding the power of identity therefore helps us understand what keeps the team together, and what pulls it apart.

By way of example I will share an experience. I worked with a team of engineers for several months, coaching the manager and working directly with the team to support their development together. The team clearly identified themselves as engineers and called themselves the engineering team. As engineers they wanted to focus on engineering and only liked involving themselves in issues that directly related to their engineering work. In particular, they distinguished themselves from 'project managers' who they actually referred to as 'them', whilst referring to the engineering team as 'us'. They worked in an 'agile' organisation where they were expected to sit wherever their work needed them to be – there were no allocated desk spaces. This would enable them to easily sit within their respective projects and close to their respective project managers. As an Extra-Dependent Team, they all worked on separate projects under different project managers so it made a great deal of sense for an agile working policy to provide the ability to sit with their respective project teams. Yet the entire engineering team insisted on sitting together in the same place in the building – deliberately separate from their respective projects. Because they had a common identity, they had a strong bond with each other and this bond meant they favoured sitting with people they *identified* with rather than the people they *worked* with.

Furthermore, the engineering team manager was resistant to changes within the organisation and did not have a strong relationship with his line manager. He described to me the reasons why this relationship wasn't strong: 'I used to work for an engineer in an engineering area. Work was relatively easy because expectations were clearer and there was more aligned knowledge. But the problem now is, I'm working for a project manager and he has a stronger view on things'. The sense of 'us' and 'them' is clearly a comparative fit that the manager used at a particular level of abstraction, limited to the boundaries of the team. What was particularly interesting about this comment was that I already knew that the line manager was actually *a qualified engineer* and not a project manager at all. The engineering team manager was using identity as a way of bonding himself with his own team whilst at the same time distancing himself from his own manager. It highlights the point that in Extra-Dependent Teams, whether they realise it or not, the sense of 'us' is generated using *similarity* and, by contrast, *difference* is used to distance 'us' from 'them'. Recognising this is key to understanding Inter-Dependent and Extra-Dependent Teams.

The power of bonding in teams

Before we explore the specifics of bonding within Inter-Dependent and Extra-Dependent Teams, let us first understand the implications of bonding power more generally. The combined power of any team can be expressed as a simple calculation:

$$1 + 1 = 2$$

Here the individual parts are bonded together to achieve the sum of the parts. In teams, this represents the minimum that would be expected. But not all bonding within teams leads to such a straightforward calculation. For example:

$$1 + 1 = 1$$

This equation indicates that the bond within the team is dysfunctional. In other words, what's happening in the team is detrimental to its expected performance. But teams are also capable of high performance – what we have already called synergy – when the total is greater than the sum of the parts. For example:

$$1 + 1 = 3$$

The possibility of synergy in teams is a major reason why teams are developed – because of the improved performance potential that it offers. But what is it that makes the bond more or less effective in teams?

I once saw a poster on a training room wall that captured this possibility in a fairly cheesy way: T.E.A.M. means Together Everyone Achieves More. That poster represents the potential power that is resident within all teams. Yet it also represents the degree of ambiguity, perhaps even ambivalence, that people in organisations have with regard to understanding what bonds teams together. Without understanding the bond that provides the power, the team in question is likely to become no better than the sum of its parts. Worse still, exerting the wrong bond between team members will lead to dysfunction and, with it, poor performance. As Peter Hawkins asks:

In what circumstances are the following true:

a) $1 + 1 + 1 + 1 + 1 + 1 = 6$
b) $1 + 1 + 1 + 1 + 1 + 1 = 2$
c) $1 + 1 + 1 + 1 + 1 + 1 = 12$

We understand '1' but do we understand '+'?

(Hawkins, 2009, p. 27)

For Hawkins, the sum is directly associated with the activity that the '+' represents. In each equation it isn't the nature of the '1' that makes the difference, but the bond of the '+'. If we do not pay attention to what binds the team together, then we do not realise the potential power of the team.

This bond is not simply a case of urging collaboration. Collaboration has too often become an end in itself when it comes to teams. As Katzenbach and Smith emphasise, performance 'is the primary objective *while a team remains the means, not the end*' (1993, p. 12, emphasis in original). So a team or manager that focuses on collaboration for its own sake in order to achieve performance synergy is at risk of making the team less effective. I will pick this up in more detail in Chapter 8 when exploring Extra-Dependent Team development. For now, let us accept that both Inter-Dependent Teams and Extra-Dependent Teams risk dysfunction but have the *potential* to achieve synergy, and that understanding and utilising the bond is crucial to the performance of the team. Teams that make use of the team bond are more likely to be effective whilst teams that resist the bond will find effectiveness an uphill struggle. This relatively simple notion is made complicated because in Inter-Dependent and Extra-Dependent Teams, this bond is very different.

The bonding power of Inter-Dependent Teams

To understand the bonding power we need to return to some of the distinctions between Inter-Dependent and Extra-Dependent Teams initially presented in Chapter 3. Firstly, let's remind ourselves of the definition of an Inter-Dependent Team:

>   Working together to achieve a common goal

The bonding power of an Inter-Dependent Team is the common goal; everyone in the team being pulled together through the existence of the single unifying goal. The Team School advocates defining the common goal of the team before knowing who will be working together to achieve that goal (Katzenbach and Smith, 1993; Wageman et al., 2008) because they understand the importance of the bond that it creates. Clarity of the common goal is therefore everything. Without a clear goal, Inter-Dependent Teams weaken their bond and with it lose their reason to be a team. Having goals that aren't common can lead to dysfunction because team members pursue different ambitions and pull the team apart. For an Inter-Dependent Team that has no clear goal, team members are likely to define their membership of the team as an end in itself; they feel like they have achieved *because* they are on the team, rather than being on the team *in order* to achieve.

Having defined a goal, an Inter-Dependent Team requires the right combination of skills needed to work together and make that goal *common* to all in the team. For Wageman et al., the first step in forming a well-composed team is, 'to ask what core skills and experience you need your team members to have if the team is to accomplish its work... Your first priority in choosing core members should be the expertise that they bring' (Wageman et al., 2008, p. 84). By definition, the goal determines the team rather than the team determining the goal.

But such skills need to be combined together between an appropriate number of team members. Too many members and they can't find the time or method to work together; too few and there wouldn't be the breadth of skills and knowledge required to achieve the goal. The correct balance of these things is determined by the goal and measured by the team's ability to be mutually accountable. Anything less than this loosens the bond within an Inter-Dependent Team.

Finally, an Inter-Dependent Team needs the willingness, commitment and trust required to work together to achieve that common goal. Lencioni's work on the five dysfunctions of teams (Lencioni, 2002) describes the necessary building blocks required within the team – from trust, through conflict, to commitment and accountability – so that the team can get the results it desires. Anything less weakens the bond and risks dysfunction and underperformance.

There are plenty of reading material, courses, videos and other resources available that describe what helps and what hinders an Inter-Dependent Team to be successful. For the purposes of this book and in service of developing the plural mental model of teams I will focus the rest of the chapter on the bond within Extra-Dependent Teams.

The bonding power of Extra-Dependent Teams

Let's remind ourselves of the definition of Extra-Dependent Teams:

> Learning together to develop a common practice

Extra-Dependent Teams therefore bond together through a common practice which consists of similar skills, techniques, knowledge, standards, interests, language, approach and problems. As we have already explored, members with the same practice can identify themselves through the similarities they have with each other – be they solicitors, midwives, salespersons, project managers or engineers – and their differences to others within the organisation – solicitors as opposed to barristers, midwives as opposed to nurses, salespersons as opposed to administrators and so on. The common practice not only defines *what* they do, but also *who* they are.

The team therefore bonds around similarity in the first instance. In the example of Malinda's team, the risk managers formed themselves into a team and bonded through their common practice. Each of them had similar skills in performing risk-management activities on behalf of their respective regions. They identified with each other because they did the same things. But they also developed that practice together and in so doing, developed their common identity through shared experience, exchanging personal stories and co-creating new ways of doing and being their practice.

Identity is also at the heart of Wenger's work. As he says, 'there is a profound connection between identity and practice' (Wenger, 1998, p. 149). Learning a practice develops a sense of social identity: what you do and who you are become interwoven. He goes on to say: 'We accumulate skills and information, not in the abstract as ends in themselves, but in the service of an identity. It is in that formation of an identity that learning can become a source of meaningfulness and of personal and social energy' (p. 215).

The similarity of identity through self-categorisation is therefore the starting point within which a common practice is built. Learning a practice creates an even stronger sense of collective identity as it combines many different factors around which a person might self-categorise. For instance, if we return to the engineering team as mentioned above, the engineers could identify with each other in terms of similar education, interests, experience, histories together, roles, project work, problems, systems, approaches, equipment and even jargon. At the same time those very same things would allow them to distinguish themselves from other practices such as project management. Whilst it may appear that the engineering team's insistence on sitting together was trivial, it was actually a practical demonstration of a sense of identity that ran much, much deeper.

Understanding the power of identity becomes even more important if we are to develop an Extra-Dependent Team and in particular if we are to be seen to lead such a team. These areas are explored fully in later chapters (see Chapters 8 and 9, respectively). But first let us understand how identity affects common practice in Extra-Dependent Teams.

The dimensions of the bond in Extra-Dependent Teams

The bond in an Extra-Dependent Team is the common practice which consists of three dimensions:

- shared repertoire;
- combined capability;
- reputation.

These dimensions build on Wenger's original dimensions of shared repertoire, joint enterprise and mutual engagement, but I have deliberately altered them to suit the formality of a managed team rather than an informal community of practice. These three dimensions acknowledge the formal structure of an Extra-Dependent Team: that they are line managed as part of a wider organisation and have stakeholders inside and outside the organisation that depend on their work. Each dimension plays an important part in understanding how an Extra-Dependent Team bonds together to perform. Misunderstanding these dimensions can encourage poor bonding, team dysfunction and inadequate performance.

Shared repertoire

The shared repertoire includes, 'routines, words, tools, ways of doing things, stories, gestures, symbols, genres, actions, or concepts that the [team] has produced or adopted in the course of its existence, and which have become part of its practice' (Wenger, 1998, p. 83). It is therefore much more than, say, a competence framework or job description. For instance, in Malinda's risk-management team the shared repertoire consisted of, amongst many other things, risk-management processes, scheduled formalised interventions, use of specialist risk-management software, stories about good and bad risk management and of course a competency framework and identical job descriptions. These all helped to form the shared repertoire.

A shared repertoire enables the members of the team to identify with each other easily, even if they rarely work together from one month to the next. The repertoire is shared between members of the team through many different channels including social interaction. For instance, turning up early to a monthly team meeting allows a casual conversation such as 'What's happening in your area?' to turn into a learning exchange between team members as they compare and contrast their work approaches, techniques and results. Both may exchange useful stories with each other and by doing so learn together and share their repertoire.

Understanding shared repertoire is not to think of it as good, bad or otherwise. Shared repertoire simply reflects what is practised amongst the team. The shared repertoire is therefore defined by the team members at any point in time as they share each other's repertoire and continually learn. It is constantly evolving and yet remains, at any point in time, the current shared repertoire of the team. If a member of the team introduces a new way of doing things, and this new way is adopted by the rest of the team, then this becomes absorbed into the shared repertoire. If a team adopts a new phrase for something that they experience, then this too becomes part of the shared repertoire. Repertoire can be shared from outside – for instance if someone picks up a new idea from an external course they attended – or generated from within the team through the conversion of their own internal knowledge (see more of this in Chapter 8). The sharing process in both cases is a process of negotiation as members learn from each other and agree the repertoire that is to be shared. This negotiation, for instance, might involve getting rid of some existing part of an individual's existing repertoire as they learn the shared repertoire, or indeed, replacing one aspect of the team's existing shared repertoire with a new technique, new process, new document or new story. Sometimes this can be a deliberate negotiation process, but often it is accidental and certainly should not be assumed to be always constructive.

A sales team that I worked with described their monthly meetings as 'The Prison'. They created this phrase to explain something they all experienced – monthly team meetings that were negative, disempowering, of no value to them *and yet* compulsory for all to attend. This is an example of the shared repertoire being negotiated between team members, 'in response to their situation and thus belongs to them in a profound sense, in spite of all the forces and influence that are beyond their control' (Wenger, 1998, p. 77). For the team, 'the prison' was real, it was theirs, it was part of the way that they did their work and it came with the role. Wenger calls this *reification* – turning an idea or notion into something real and concrete. By naming the sales team meeting 'The Prison', it became a real and unique part of their shared repertoire. It was passed onto newcomers to the team with as much meaning as any other important part of the job.

Over time, the shared repertoire builds and maintains the collective history of the practice. Old techniques and language invented by team members who have long since left, survive staff turnover even though new members don't know the techniques' origins and new elements of the shared repertoire are adopted to suit the changing requirements of organisational stakeholders. Each team member picks up the meaning within the shared repertoire and makes it their own. If, for instance the sales team example above completely changed all its members, the new members might still call monthly team meetings 'The Prison'. Shared repertoire holds meaning for what it is to be part of the team.

Whist the repertoire is *shared* across the team it isn't necessarily *identical* – team members are not clones and so there is always going to be some individual differences in the way that the shared repertoire is applied. Some people are new to the team and learn as quickly as possible how the specifics of the shared repertoire are done 'around here'. By contrast, other team members may have been in post for a long time and learned not only how to do things well, but also how to take short-cuts and make what they do look easy. Variations across a shared repertoire are to be expected within an Extra-Dependent Team and they do not affect the way that the team identifies with their similarities. Whilst one team member might be a relative novice in their use of the repertoire and others in the team are masters by comparison, their common practice and shared identity together maintains their bond. The combination of their shared repertoire is known as the combined capability.

Combined capability

The output of an Extra-Dependent Team is its *combined capability*. The combined capability consists of each individual team member's repertoire and reflects the impact of the bond and its effectiveness on performance. Where an Extra-Dependent Team shares its repertoire amongst the team it improves each and every individual's ability to deliver. For instance, in a sales team, a salesperson uses their individual repertoire to sell in order to hit an individual target. If they sell particularly well they might exceed the target, reflecting a high capability. Should others in the team pick up and use the successful techniques of their colleague the shared repertoire would improve everyone's individual capability. The improvement reflects the combination of the shared repertoire across the team. The combined capability of the team is therefore not only found within each individual team member, but also within the whole team. If members of the team are all improving their ability to sell, the team's output is greater than it was before.

Teams that share their repertoire collectively benefit mutually and are more likely to improve their combined capability and thus drive individual and team performance which directly serves the team's dependent stakeholders outside the team. If salespeople sell more products, more products need to be made, delivered and billed. An improved combined capability can have a multiplier effect on a whole organisation.

It makes for a compelling reason to share repertoire with each other. Everyone realises the mutual benefit of doing so. If I learn from you and you learn from me, we are better together. Such learning leads to sustainable improvements in the performance of the team. And such improvements have a positive and strategic impact on the whole organisation as each person is a fractal of the whole team. As a result, the team's reputation is in each and every team member's hands.

Reputation

Reputation is the factor we have explored so far most closely associated with identity. Reputation isn't a team nickname or team motto, neither is it a vision statement, although it can involve any or none of these things. Reputation is how the team identifies with itself combined with the way those who depend on the team identify it. Reputation is therefore always present – whether the team wishes it or not. It could be that a team has a reputation for high-quality and strong delivery; but equally a team might be invisible to all but a few people in the organisation and therefore have a discreet, perhaps undervalued reputation. Reputations, and by definition identity, can therefore be changed – from what it was to what one desires it to be. If a team achieves synergy in its combined capability the reputation might change from being an adequate team to being a performing team.

But to achieve a reputation across the team, there needs to be a clear, strong and consistent sense of 'us'. As we have explored already, the common practice within the team is a strong identifying bond from the outset. Yet identifying inside the team is not enough. Individual members work directly with people outside of the team and these relationships are the ones that provide the outside-in reputation. Many Extra-Dependent Teams have separate accountabilities with unique individuals. If we return to the real example of Malinda's risk management team, for example, each team member had a separate region to work to, each with a different regional director and regional leadership team. In this case team reputation was channelled through the respective individual. If the regional risk manager was very good, then the reputation of the whole team might be seen to be very good. If the regional risk manager was struggling to deliver, then the reputation of the team took a hit.

From the inside out, an Extra-Dependent Team's reputation needs to be transmitted outside the team as a sense of 'us' rather than a sense of 'me'. In Extra-Dependent Teams that share repertoire and improve their combined capability, this sense of 'us' is stronger. It can be too easy in situations where outside stakeholders experience only one team member, for that team member to think more like 'me' than 'we' and therefore seek to develop an individual reputation rather than to acknowledge that they represent the team reputation. After all, the way that they work locally is their responsibility and accountability. But the power of identity is also seen from the outside – the outside stakeholders see the bond in the Extra-Dependent Team. Even though a regional leadership team only experiences one risk manager, they know that that risk manager is part of a wider risk team. When an Extra-Dependent Team member attempts to establish an individual reputation, it automatically reflects on the team reputation: 'They are a bunch of individuals'; 'There is no consistency'; 'They have a silo mentality'; 'They don't get on well together'. The point is that with the power of 'us', the 'we' is always present – from the inside and the outside.

The bond in the double 0s

To bring some sort of context to the shared repertoire, the combined capability and the team reputation, I will illustrate with an example of an Extra-Dependent Team that many people will know of, but few will have really considered. Ian Fleming's James Bond is code-named Double 0 Seven. He is one of a number of Double 0s that report to M. It is only implied in the films, but each Double 0 operates independently on spy missions working alongside contacts in the field and HQ personnel such as Q, who provides them with various gadgets. They are, by structure, an Extra-Dependent Team. But what is their shared repertoire, their combined capability and their team reputation?

We cannot be sure what the shared repertoire is amongst the Double 0 team because they are never seen together. But it is suggested by what James Bond himself does. Some things he does are unique to him whilst other aspects can be inferred to be shared across the whole team. The team's shared repertoire includes:

*   being licenced to kill;
*   being able to use many different weapons;
*   working independently as a field agent (James Bond's tendency is to be more independent than M might wish!);
*   being unflappable in high-velocity situations;
*   being intellectually razor-sharp;
*   having a history of audacious and heroic successes to overthrow ascending megalomaniacs;
*   using quick-witted clichés (James Bond uses 'Bond, James Bond', 'shaken, not stirred' and his humorous quips after killing someone – other Double 0s would use their own);
*   mastering various new spy gadgets within a few seconds and then using them in the field with devastating effect.

Sadly, the adventure and excitement of the stories means that we don't get to find out how this repertoire is shared amongst the team. No doubt it involves post-mission report writing, team meetings, perhaps even mentoring of new team members. Whilst such things can seem unexciting in the context of James Bond, if the repertoire was shared more often amongst the team members, perhaps James Bond would have a greater sense of 'us' and not be such a difficult team member for M to manage. We're back to herding cats.

The Double 0s' combined capability can be defined as the close-quarter disruption of criminal and terrorist activity that, wherever it is in the world, threatens British interests. The team size might need to increase or decrease according to the nature of the threat of such criminal or terrorist activity. This combined capability might also increase as new techniques are learned by the Double 0s. We assume that James Bond is the ideal Double 0 – why would we watch a film about the second best? If the amazing capability of James Bond could be shared with the other Double 0s in the team, per-haps he wouldn't *always* be the one who had to save the world! Of course, it wouldn't make for a good story, but it would increase the team's combined capability to disrupt criminal and terrorist activity. It might also reduce some of the risk and stress that James Bond experiences!

Lastly, the Double 0 team has (ironically for a team of spies) a global rep-utation. Within the team they will be self-assured expert killing machines. Internal to their organisation, they are more likely to be known as difficult, arrogant, yet indispensable and highly effective. Both perspectives align to build a reputation within the team and a sense of 'us' as compared to 'them'. Their identity is cemented by some of their distinctive shared repertoire – tuxedos and handguns, armoured sportscars and the Double 0 itself.

Similarity, difference and team dysfunction

By way of concluding this chapter I will highlight the importance of rec-ognising the difference between bonding around difference and bonding around similarity. When managers of Inter-Dependent Teams don't define a common goal, their team has nothing to bond itself around. Their differ-ences are likely to cause dysfunction as they are able to work separately for their own purposes, only to point the finger at someone else as the reason why they weren't able to achieve what they wanted to achieve. The common goal should unite them and ensure their differences are combined and their disagreements are constructive, because they are all mutually accountable.

But a common goal would have the opposite impact for an Extra-Dependent Team. A common goal in an Extra-Dependent Team will divert team members' attention away from the very people that they need to work with outside the team, thereby making their ability to deliver the combined capability much harder. When an Extra-Dependent Team seeks to utilise their differences, they start to depend on each other to deliver together what should be delivered individually. The team becomes imbalanced and inconsistent, with each member only able to deliver part of the shared repertoire rather than all of it. The team therefore changes its relationship with stakeholders so that rather than one person dealing with them, they all need to deal with them. To the stakeholders it's heavy-handed and makes for more effort which starts to affect reputation, which in turn impacts the dynamics in the team. The team doesn't find it easy to work with itself and becomes dysfunctional and underachieves.

In contrast, an Extra-Dependent Team manager that focuses on common *practice* ensures that the strengths of each individual team member's repertoire is shared for the benefit of all within the team, thus addressing weaknesses and inconsistencies and thereby increasing the combined capability of the team as a whole. Such moves help build performance and the positive reputation of the team as an integral, strategically important part of the organisation.

By Extra-Dependent Team managers focusing on similarity and Inter-Dependent Team managers focusing on difference, the whole organisation is therefore more strongly bonded together.

References

Haslam, S A, van Knippenberg, D, Platow, M J and Ellemers, N (2003) *Social Identity at Work: Developing Theory for Organizational Practice*, Psychology Press, Hove.

Haslam, S A, Reicher, S D and Platow, M J (2011) *The New Psychology of Leadership: Identity, Influence and Power*, Psychology Press, Hove.

Hawkins, P (2009) *Coaching and Consulting: Where Next?* Institute of Business Consulting Conference, self-published.

Katzenbach, J and Smith, D (1993) *The Wisdom of Teams: Creating the High-Performance Organization*, Harvard Business School Press, Harvard, MA.

Lencioni, P (2002) The *Five Dysfunctions of a Team*, Jossey-Bass, San Francisco.

Wageman, R, Nunes, D A, Burruss, J A and Hackman, J R (2008) *Senior Leadership Teams*, Harvard Business School Press, Harvard, MA.

Wenger, E (1998) *Communities of Practice: Learning, Meaning and Identity*, Cambridge University Press, New York.

5 Extra-Dependent Team dynamics

Unless the dynamics of an Extra-Dependent Team are understood, a manager will not appreciate what lies behind the behaviours that they witness, nor understand their own part in those dynamics. It is very important that everyone in the team, including the manager, appreciates that they play an influential role in how the team works, together and apart, to achieve synergy or indeed when causing dysfunction.

I therefore return to the excellent work of Etienne Wenger and others on understanding communities of practice (Lave and Wenger, 1991; Wenger, 1998; Wenger et al., 2002; Hughes et al., 2007; McDermott and Archibald, 2010) as well as continuing to access the work on Social Identity Theory (Haslam et al., 2003, 2011) in order to appreciate what goes on in Extra-Dependent Teams.

Practice, identity and learning

As we have already heard in previous chapters, Wenger makes the case that practice and identity are profoundly connected. Furthermore, he argues that the development of a practice, individually and communally, is done through the social process of learning. It is learning a practice – the specific language to use, skills, behaviours, unique equipment, how to engage with each other, when to do things, when not to do other things – that enables us to connect with others similar to ourselves with whom we share an identity:

> Membership in a community of practice translates into an identity as a form of competence. An identity in this sense is relating to the world as a particular mix of the familiar and the foreign... In practice, we know who we are by what is familiar, understandable, usable, negotiable: we know who we are not by what is foreign, opaque, unwieldy, unproductive.
> (Wenger, 1998, p. 153)

The dynamics that drive Extra-Dependent Teams therefore revolve around learning about and identity with the practice. These dynamics consist of layers, prototypicality, learning trajectories and the interplay between new-comers and elders.

Layers in Extra-Dependent Teams

There are three layers in Extra-Dependent Teams similar to the concentric circles identified in communities of practice in organisations (Wenger et al., 2002). These layers represent the degree to which the team members are expert in the common practice.

The layers are called Core, Active and Peripheral (see Figure 5.1). The Peripheral layer is typically occupied by those who are new to the team and are learning the practice. By contrast, inside the Core layer reside members of the team considered to be experts in this common practice. They are the role models for others in the team. The Active layer contains team members who sit between Core and Peripheral layers. They are active participants in the common practice of the team, using it to good effect, but still have much to learn and much to offer.

The closer to the centre of the layers a team member is, the more a team member represents what it is to be an expert in the team's common practice. The idea of normative fit within the in-group returns here. Haslam et al. (2011) recognise that within groups of similarities there is an expectation of how people will talk and behave within that group. This is a process of fitting in, of learning the practice and being part of the in-group. Those at the centre of the circles – right at the centre of the Core layer – are what Haslam et al. describe as category *prototypes*. They represent the *very essence* of what it is to be in that in-group, wielding the full shared repertoire, applying the combined capability and embodying the reputation of the team. Prototypicality epitomises the identity of the team and represents what makes 'us' so different from 'them'.

By way of example, let us return to the Double 0 team. Ian Fleming's James Bond character is the very essence of what being a Double 0 is all about.

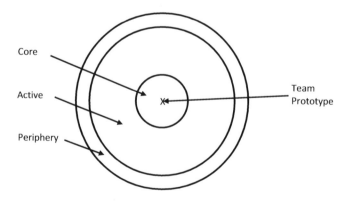

Figure 5.1 The layers in Extra-Dependent Teams.

His daring character oozes out into a gambling habit, his confidence in his ability stretches so far that he often announces himself to his rival by his full name, and not only does he learn to use the random gadgets he is given, he masters them within seconds. He therefore represents prototypicality in the Double 0 team. To those inside the team he is someone to emulate. For those outside the team he is superhuman and utterly distinct.

We will look at the importance of prototypicality in more detail in Chapter 9. For now, it makes a good reference point for exploring each of the three layers that radiate from that point and understanding how that affects dynamics in the team.

Core layer

Team members that occupy the Core layer are recognised as role models for the team. The shared repertoire of the team is effectively held by its Core members. They are the ones who embody expertise in the practice, they utilise the full range of language, master the systems and processes involved and accomplish work with the appearance and behaviour that exemplify the skills of the practitioner. Because of their expertise, Core members are also likely to be high achievers. With regards to teams' combined capability, they are likely to be able to deliver the higher levels of performance compared to others in the team. This capability might be in terms of quantity or quality, but it also might be in terms of complexity or sheer difficulty.

Because of all these factors, they wield power within the team. Others less capable are influenced by their expertise and see them as senior. Indeed, in many Extra-Dependent Teams Core members are given the name 'senior' – senior lecturer, senior consultant, senior nurse, etc. This language reflects a differentiated identity and further builds the power of Core members giving them disproportionate influence over the team. For instance, their voice will be more influential than others in the team when it comes to setting standards of practice, monitoring skill levels, changing processes, defining priority agendas within the team, deciding on the pace and direction of innovations and setting the tone in terms of who 'we' are, compared to 'them'.

Core members are also the people most likely to act as a spokesperson for the team. They speak confidently from their own experience and point of view, whilst accurately representing the essence of the team's common practice. Their seniority, influence and power enable Core members to be heard by 'them' outside the team so that the team is noticed, its place in the wider system is made relevant and the common practice of the team is seen to matter. Of course, such influence shapes the team's reputation. To those inside the team, Core members championing the team represent the identity of the team – what 'we' are about. To those outside the team, a Core member represents what is different about the practice and influences expectations about what is possible from the combined capability. Core members disproportionately shape team reputation.

Peripheral layer

Let's now move from the Core to the Periphery as it helps understand the extremes of layers in the team. People occupying the Peripheral layer of the team are typically (but not exclusively) new members. As a new member it is legitimate not to know everything there is to know about the common practice. New team members need induction, familiarisation and acclimatisation within the team. They might be partnered with a mentor from elsewhere in the team – someone to learn from, to copy, to ask questions of and to pick up the local 'dialect' of the practice. This early learning process in the Peripheral layer is expected to be a transition from whatever they used to do, to soon being fully incumbent of the team's common practice.

But the closer to the outer edge a Peripheral member is, the less like 'us' the person is. The Peripheral layer therefore also accommodates team members leaving the team. This might be fleeting as a highly respected team member works their notice and hands over their responsibilities to others, rapidly shedding their identity as 'one of us'. Alternatively, it could be more gradual as a team member moves towards retirement, gradually reducing their hours and with it their sense of belonging within the team. It is important to remember that it is entirely appropriate to be a member of the team and in the Peripheral layer. Lave and Wenger originally called this 'legitimate peripheral participation' (Lave and Wenger, 1991). For team dynamics, it is really important to appreciate people when they join and leave. So realising when team members are in the Peripheral layer is an important acknowledgement of how they are learning and how they identify with the team. Indeed, as we will see later, some team members can linger too long within the Peripheral layer and that can often be causal or symptomatic of other issues within the team.

Active layer

Between the Core and the Peripheral layers is the Active layer made up of everyone else in the team. Active team members are full participants in the common practice. They are well versed in the shared repertoire and will be aware of when they comply with it and when they do not. It could be expected that most team members will be in this layer.

Active members are most likely to be people who mentor newcomers because they are more likely to identify with each other as compared to a Core member mentoring. An Active member therefore represents the short-term learning destination for a new team member and constitutes becoming a full member of the team – fitting in. Active members also know the local rules for operating the common practice and are able to share these informally with the new team member to suit their needs.

Active members may themselves have aspirations for being a Core member and may be close to the edge of the Core layer. Such Active members might be auxiliary to Core members, providing close support and assistance without quite meeting the standards of occupants of the Core layer. In return the Core member may act as mentor to the Active member, helping them to learn to become a Core member themselves. To bring this to life, let's see how it works in a real example. We'll return to the engineering team first mentioned in Chapter 3.

Case study part 1

Erik was head of engineering within a construction organisation. He had a team of five senior project engineers (SPEs), each of whom provided specialist engineering advice to different construction projects from start to finish. Erik allocated which SPE would work on which projects. All SPEs worked on different projects.

Erik had been in post for nearly a year and had struggled to recruit and retain good engineers. He knew that the team was made up of a mix of abilities. There were some top-class engineers but there were others who, whilst they knew their subject, were less effective due to poor self-organising, negative personal skills or just being difficult to manage. Erik was conscious that this inconsistency was having a negative effect on the reputation of the team from project managers and others.

Erik assessed the team using the three layers (see Figure 5.2).

Colin – Mid-Active

Colin was OK at engineering, a safe pair of hands, but very disorganised in terms of communication and time management. Erik found he had to support Colin a lot to ensure he met the project managers' expectations of him.

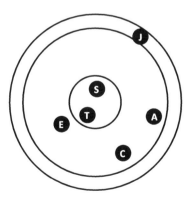

Figure 5.2 Plotting an Extra-Dependent Team into the layers.

Tony – Core

Tony had a very strong individual reputation. He was very experienced in this area, was personable, energetic and clear with what engineering could do and what it could not. Erik would often run ideas and plans past Tony before sharing them with the rest of the team. Eric received solid, clear council from Tony. Tony also had his ear to the ground and knew everyone in the team better than anyone.

Sally – Core

Sally was good at engineering and was also very organised. She was a reliable SPE who could easily be left to work on her own. Because of this, Erik would sometimes use Sally's strength to support projects that had less experienced project managers in charge. Sally would provide additional help and guidance, which was appreciated.

Ashni – Low Active

Ashni was very capable as an engineer, but she was a contractor on a rolling contract, rather than a permanent employee. Whilst Ashni could be relied upon to do a good engineering job, she didn't show any interest in doing much more, including understanding the wider organisational issues. As a result, Erik often left Ashni out of team meetings and rarely spent much time with her.

Jim – Peripheral

Jim was widely recognised as very difficult to work with, but always seemed to do a good job for the project managers who depended on his work. His interpersonal skills were at best mediocre, at worst rude. Erik had learned not to put Jim as a lead on a project, but to use him in a pure engineering role – to provide answers and advice where required. Jim was over retirement age, showed little interest in his career, the organisation or others in his team. Even so, his work was consistently of a high standard and he had been in the team as long as anyone could remember.

Erik – high Active

As for Erik himself, he had a lot of experience in engineering, but tended to be absorbed in management issues. Since joining he had focused his attention on recruitment and hadn't really had much time to settle fully into the team. As a result, he relied heavily on Tony to get the inside story on the team and also as reassurance on his decision making.

Applying this information, albeit limited, to the three layers, you are likely to get something like Figure 5.2. On the face of it we have a team that has two Core members who set the standard for the team, one Peripheral member who is experienced but very challenging and the rest Active members, including the team manager himself. To these layers we now need to add learning trajectories.

Learning trajectories

As has already been inferred through the learning of new people joining, Extra-Dependent Team members do not remain static within these three layers. Each team member will have their own individual learning trajectory which represents their learning history, where they are now and where they are headed. There are four principal trajectories (Figure 5.3; I explore the notion of a fifth type of trajectory in Chapter 10).

Inbound

The inbound trajectory captures a team member moving towards prototypicality. This learning trajectory is very much about becoming a member of the team. It's about seeing oneself and being seen by others to become what it is to be the essence of the practice. For inbound Peripheral team members, it might initially involve learning some specific skills, understanding the local jargon or demonstrating that they are moving up the competency scores. For inbound Active team members, this means showing a good rate of learning around the shared repertoire, really mastering the essentials as well as stretching towards the more challenging aspects of the common practice. For an inbound Core member, it demonstrates a concentration of mastery, a continual thirst to better oneself, as well as a desire to develop the future potential of the common practice. Inbound trajectories can be rapid or can take years, depending on the pace of learning.

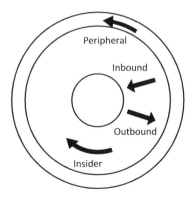

Figure 5.3 Plotting an Extra-Dependent Team's trajectories.

Outbound

Conversely, a team member increasingly going about things in their own way, in contrast to the team's common practice, is on an outbound trajectory. This isn't just a case of being flexible with the common practice, adapting it to local requirements. An outbound trajectory would mean someone was finding it hard to use shared repertoire to do their work and thus was turning to other methods to get things done. Such methods might be seen to be contrary to what 'we' do and therefore more likely to be something that 'they' did. Becoming less like 'us' and more like 'them' is indicative of an outbound trajectory.

Individuals struggling to perform might also be on an outbound trajectory. They may know their professional skills, but they might not be learning how to apply it 'here'. The common practice of the Extra-Dependent Team is specific to context – the context of the organisation they are part of – and so just being good at something doesn't necessarily mean that a team member can engage with others in the organisation to apply their repertoire appropriately. An outbound trajectory can be a difficult thing to reverse because of the impact on identity. Outbound team members increasingly lose engagement with in-group colleagues and become correspondingly more isolated within the team. This disengagement makes it difficult to provide the support needed to help turn the person around.

Where two or more team members are sharing an outbound trajectory, it is likely that they find common identity with the experience and seek comfort from each other to make sense of their changing fortunes. Such a concentration of people within a team can become problematic as they find their confidence to speak out about their experience. If not handled well, such issues can split teams. That being said, anyone leaving the team to move onto another role, even something as positive as promotion, will take an outbound trajectory. As I have said, leaving the team is something to acknowledge and manage well.

Insider

Insiders are generally content to remain relatively stable where they are. They will learn enough to broaden their repertoire and keep pace of change, but have neither the appetite to take an inbound trajectory nor wish to risk an outbound trajectory. An insider doesn't have to be a permanent trajectory. It could simply be a pause to consolidate some rapid learning having recently joined the team. It might be that the workload is such that just standing still is as much as can be achieved.

But insiders are still learning. The team as a whole will be undergoing a degree of change to maintain its position within the wider context of the organisation. Perhaps new objectives for the neighbouring Inter-Dependent Teams are demanding more from each team member, meaning that the Extra-Dependent Team needs to alter its repertoire to match. Alternatively, the organisation might have introduced a new IT system, a new cyber security policy, altered the expenses policy or even merged with another organisation, all of which require the team to readjust elements of its shared repertoire in order to maintain its combined capability and preserve its reputation.

Peripheral

Finally, the peripheral trajectory is similar to the insider trajectory, but it is uniquely relevant to the Peripheral layer. It might typically be a trajectory for a new team member who finds it difficult to get 'inside' the team: they may be a team member in name, but they have yet to find a way to learn how to become a member of the team, what the full shared repertoire is and how that represents the common practice. They might have little access to other team members and therefore have little opportunity to learn. Alternatively, they might not identify with other members of the team, choosing to keep their distance whilst they decide what to do.

A peripheral trajectory might also be taken by someone who had been on an outbound trajectory but didn't quite leave the team. Such a person might skulk about on the fringes of the team, being a member in name, but practising their own repertoire, independent of the shared practice. Their independence allows them to continue, sometimes little noticed, struggling to find alternative options for their specialist skills. Indecision and inaction by the manager and other team members leaves them there for longer.

It is no doubt clear that whilst an insider trajectory is healthy and purposeful in its own right, the peripheral trajectory is likely to indicate problems. The peripheral trajectory is neither deciding to become more like 'us' nor to become more like 'them'. It's likely to be a lonely place for the individual concerned and therefore unhealthy for the individual as much as it is for others in the team. The longer it lasts, the more troublesome it is likely to get.

Case study part 2

We can apply these trajectory types to each of the engineering team members (Figure 5.4).

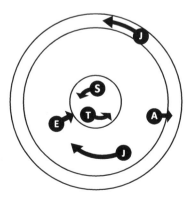

Figure 5.4 The engineering team's dynamics.

Colin – Insider

Colin had strengths and weaknesses in his practice as a senior project engineer in this team in this organisation. Whilst he was a competent engineer, he needed support in organisational skills. He was therefore working to tread water in the Active layer.

Tony – Insider

Tony was the most prototypical member of the engineering team. He had the skills, experience, jargon, assertiveness, contacts, history and physical 'presence' of what it was to be an engineer. He continued to develop his repertoire as an engineer, but only enough to keep the status quo, so plots an insider trajectory.

Sally – Insider

Sally's solid engineering and organisational skills meant she was learning to deal with more inexperienced project managers, thus helping to develop relationships if not the techniques of engineering. But such techniques were isolated from the rest of the team, so she was therefore on an insider trajectory.

Ashni – Outbound

Ashni's contractor status meant she saw herself as only a temporary member of the team. On its own this might have made her an insider as she learned enough to do the role. But Erik's decisions to leave her out of team conversations about broader issues because of her contractor status meant that she was slowly being edged out of the team. It's a slow outbound trajectory.

I would argue that it didn't have to be that way should the team and the contractor realise the benefits of acting as a regular member of the team. But it was Erik's assumption that Ashni's contractor status would mean a lack of engagement in broader organisational issues and ironically Erik's actions ensured Ashni's outbound trajectory behaviour reflected his assumption.

Jim – Peripheral

Jim's behaviour was poor and far from that expected of a senior project engineer. But he wasn't learning how to leave the team either. Even though he could retire, neither he nor Erik was broaching the issue of bringing him back into the Active layer or helping him to exit the team for something different (be that retirement, another job or something else). This meant he was stuck on the outside on a peripheral trajectory.

Erik – Inbound

Erik learned to copy Tony and was on an inbound trajectory. Without realising it, Erik used Tony's prototypicality to influence the team: he checked ideas and decisions with Tony before sharing them with the rest of the team. Tony also knew that his own Core status and power was amplified through his close association with the manager.

These examples help to demonstrate how the layers and trajectories combined to enable team members to appreciate their dynamics and therefore consider what can be done to manage them differently. This latter point is covered in the following four chapters. But before then, there is one last dynamic that plays out in Extra-Dependent Teams: newcomers and elders.

Elders

The elders in an Extra-Dependent Team are those team members who have been around longer than most. Because of this they have experienced the changing history of the common practice and are able to share stories and experiences about how things were or weren't different. This history provides a source of influence within the team in a number of ways. Firstly, they have access to information about the common practice that few others have. They can therefore be a useful source for the team, to better understand what happened in the past to get the team to where it is today. Secondly, their history can access data that aren't easily found elsewhere; information on why changes happened the way they did, what it felt like at certain points or telling stories of heroes and villains in the practice that caused the shared repertoire to be successful or unsuccessful at different times. Such historical data help explain to non-elders in the team the way that the common practice has been shaped, what demands can be made on the common practice by others in the system and how that has changed over time. Finally, because very few people know about these histories, the Elder can use their knowledge of the history of the practice in a selective way, using it to put a particular perspective on events, 'It wasn't like this in my day', 'People used to have more/less respect for us', 'It was because of such-and-such that we're in this predicament now'. So the act of accessing or eliciting such historical information from elders has to be done with care and consideration.

Because of their team longevity elders have had time to master the common practice, even to develop it further. They can therefore often be found in the Core layer of an Extra-Dependent Team. They make intuitive role models for others in the team as they represent a simple inbound trajectory from apprentice to master over time. But the Core layer is not always where Elders are to be found, and sometimes what should be an intuitive role model becomes a more challenging dynamic within the team.

Some elders don't ever get to the Core layer, but instead are content to remain in the Active layer doing enough to stay but lacking the desire, capability or prominence to move into the Core layer. Nonetheless, such elders can play an important part in the team – as mentors for newcomers for instance – and by being reliable contributors to the combined capability. But should an elder refrain from continuous improvement or not keep up to date with changes within the repertoire to match the changing needs of the organisation, they begin to slip out of the Active layer and they become outbound.

Elders that are found on the Peripheral layer can be problematic. In the engineer team case study, Jim is such an elder in the Peripheral layer. He was sufficiently competent to keep his job, but he was also non-collaborative to the point of rudeness making him a real challenge for any manager. Given that Erik was in the Active layer himself and a little reliant on Tony for comfort, it meant that he was indecisive and insufficiently assertive with Jim. Jim was therefore left to stagnate on the edge of the team, not really being a full member and not really being able to leave. Perhaps he had 'belonged' too long? Perhaps he didn't know what to do 'out there' once he had left the team and retired? But for everyone concerned it was dysfunctional for Jim to remain neither 'in' nor 'out'.

Newcomers

The opposite end of the practice lifecycle are the newcomers. Newcomers are typically found within the Periphery layer because they have quite literally just joined the team. A newcomer on an inbound trajectory will rapidly learn the shared repertoire from mentors in the team, including elders. In the Peripheral layer they feel the freedom to ask the 'stupid question' that those in the Active and Core layers find much harder to ask. The quicker they learn, the steeper the inbound trajectory and the sooner they enter the Active layer.

But the individuals themselves, indeed others in the team, too, might still consider them a newcomer – not quite a full member of the team. It might take months, even years depending on the turnover of team members, for a newcomer to feel like a full member of the team – one of 'us' – especially if they remain the last newcomer to the team.

Other team members play a part in this slow integration into the team. Internal friendships by other Active members, longer-term relationships between Core members and other similar dynamics such as Erik's dependency on Tony mean that the existing team members may not be very accommodating to the newcomer. So the situation is similar to the elder in the Periphery: a newcomer in the Active layer is symptomatic of wider dynamics within the team.

Not everyone in the team is either a newcomer or an elder, but these polarised types of team members are worth noting because they have an important interplay relationship which can help or hinder the common practice of the Extra-Dependent Team.

Elders versus newcomers

The learning dynamic between elders and newcomers is vital to the success of the team. Newcomers learn quickly from elders, allowing them to pick up the shared repertoire as quickly as possible. By picking up that shared repertoire they are more likely to contribute a fair share of the combined capability. The quicker this process happens the greater the consistency across the team and therefore the more consistent the reputation that the team has. But it is not a one-way street of learning. Elders can learn from the shared repertoire of newcomers. Newcomers can challenge the existing shared repertoire, asking difficult questions about the way things are done and why it happens the way it does. Extra-Dependent Teams that cultivate learning within them welcome such questions and challenges seeking to combine the new with the old to generate an enhanced shared repertoire.

But sometimes elders are defensive of such questions. They seek to use their history of the shared practice in order to explain why things are as they are and why the newcomer needs to conform, rather than explore the thinking and experience behind the question and use the outside knowledge of the newcomer to the benefit of the current shared repertoire. After all, newcomers have previous repertoire of the practice – it is what made them 'similar' enough to be recruited into the team in the first place. Too often in Extra-Dependent Teams the experience and knowledge that got the newcomer into the team is discarded on entry in favour of the team's existing shared repertoire. By the time the newcomer has learned that they can offer an alternative to the shared repertoire, they have become too integrated, just want to fit in or have perhaps lost touch with what they used to do and now find themselves too clumsy to share in this new team.

Reality check

The layers and the trajectories combine to create a simple yet compelling way for the dynamics within Extra-Dependent Teams to be acknowledged for what they are. Plotting team members into the three layers, identifying their learning trajectories and whether they might be a newcomer or elder is not an act of aspiration – it is not helpful to plot where you *want* members to be. Plotting is about recognising the reality of each person's situation, their actions, interactions and reactions. One plots the team *as it is*. By understanding the dynamics within an Extra-Dependent Team people in the team, including the manager, can identify choices and ways forward for individuals and the team collectively. Only by identifying with Erik the engineering manager, that Jim was an elder on the Periphery of the team, did Erik then discover that he had choices he hadn't previously seen. Erik had thought that Jim was very difficult to manage, but too precious to let go. When Erik identified the reality of where Jim was it was clear that Erik had two options: to invest his management time and skill to help bring Jim back into the team or to talk to Jim about his future outside the team. This wouldn't be an easy conversation to be had – either way. But doing nothing wasn't helping anyone. Within a month, Jim had retired.

Understanding the dynamics helps a manager develop options and take choices for dealing with performance, development and leadership of the team. Dynamics helps to appreciate that with Extra-Dependent Teams, the practice of management is very different.

References

Haslam, S, van Knippenberg, D, Platow, M J and Ellemers, N (2003) *Social Identity at Work: Developing Theory for Organizational Practice*, Psychology Press, Hove.

Haslam, S A, Reicher, S D and Platow, M J (2011) *The New Psychology of Leadership: Identity, Influence and Power*, Psychology Press, Hove.

Hughes, J Jewson, N and Unwin, L (2007) *Communities of Practice: Critical Perspectives*, Routledge, London.

Lave, J and Wenger, E (1991) *Situated Learning: Legitimate Peripheral Participation*, Cambridge University Press, New York.

McDermott, R and Archibald, D (2010) Harnessing Your Staff's Informal Networks, *Harvard Business Review*, March.

Wenger, E (1998) *Communities of Practice: Learning, Meaning and Identity*, Cambridge University Press, New York.

Wenger, E, McDermott, R and Snyder, W M (2002) *Cultivating Communities of Practice: A Guide to Managing Knowledge*, Harvard Business School Publishing, Boston, MA.

6 Extra-Dependent Team management

The main challenge for a manager of an Extra-Dependent Team is to recognise that, whilst the power of 'us' binds the team together, it is with 'them' that performance is delivered. The Extra-Dependent Team manager must constantly work to build the capability that helps deliver performance elsewhere in the organisation. On their own, Extra-Dependent Teams cannot deliver anything. They must work with other people outside of the team. Each individual member of an Extra-Dependent Team needs to work interdependently with other people in order to apply their specialist practice in a meaningful manner. Salespeople cannot perform without working with the people who make what they sell; risk managers need an operation that takes risks; engineers cannot engineer without a project which requires engineering.

On the face of it, it's a paradoxical position – to manage a team of people, who don't work with each other, but instead can only perform with others outside of the team, and yet it is the manager who is accountable for that team. It sounds ridiculous, but it's happening throughout organisations throughout the world right now. And the conventional mental model of teams assesses such conditions as dysfunctional. It does little to help tackle some of the unique challenges associated with managing an Extra-Dependent Team because of the following reasons.

1   It's not like managing an Inter-Dependent Team.
2   The accountability is disproportionately borne on the shoulders of the manager.
3   Empowerment is not a choice, it's a necessity.
4   The manager is often also a practitioner.
5   Constructive conflict works differently.
6   The common practice is often influenced by professional bodies remote from the organisation.

What do these challenges mean for managers of Extra-Dependent Teams? Basically, it means leading such a team is tricky. What will make the difference for a manager is what mental model is used to think about the team because this perspective will provide choices that either help to build the team and its performance or hinder it by adding further complications.

The pitfalls of managing Extra-Dependent Teams

When tasked with managing an Extra-Dependent Team managers make a number of choices that fit, generally speaking, into the first two levels of the mental model outlined in Chapter 2:

Level 1 – Best guess
Level 2 – Team or group

This is because until now, only the first two levels have been available to managers of Extra-Dependent Teams. The role of manager is therefore prejudiced towards existing ways of seeing teams and groups and the choices for managers are limited. We will explore these in detail below before appreciating what it takes to be a manager of an Extra-Dependent Team when both types of teams are acknowledged and the challenges listed above are addressed. This relates to the plural mental model of teams:

Level 3 – Inter-Dependent Team AND Extra-Dependent Team

Best guess management

Best guess management principally falls into two extremes – management through competitiveness and management through collaboration. Both I will explore below before highlighting a third type which tends to appear when the manager is exhausted by the previous two – management by exception.

Competition

In my experience working with and studying teams made up of similar roles the default approach that managers adopt is to stimulate competitiveness within the team. This competitiveness is driven by the belief that rivalry motivates people to perform better. The thinking goes: someone who is beaten to the top by a colleague will come back fighting which will mean both improve; thus the sum is greater than the parts. Team members are susceptible to competitiveness because their comparable goals provide something against which to compete. It makes for a strange dynamic analogous to sibling rivalry: each of them wishes to out-do the other whilst simultaneously being bonded through common identity.

Management in a team of sibling rivals is both frustrating and strangely familiar. It is frustrating in that whilst the logic of competition should return dividends, the reality is that winners in the team are always completely outnumbered by losers. And the ratings don't change that much. Star players remain star players whilst poor performers remain poor performers. The energy involved in dealing with the rivalry makes the manager question the gains made. So why does it perpetuate?

The manager may feel entirely at home with such a situation as it resembles other group dynamics that they may be familiar with such as their domestic circumstances or amateur sports teams. The manager can gain great comfort from the validation of their powerful position that wields the ability to award the winner, rebuke the losers and even disqualify cheats. It's a divide-and-rule approach which leaves the team fighting with each other for the manager's patronage.

But it's got nothing to do with managing a team as all this time the promised synergy remains elusive. As a recent report by the Chartered Management Institute highlights, 'There is no consistent relationship between competition and performance... This seems to be the case in most settings but is especially apt for contexts where teamwork or collaboration are important' (Chartered Management Institute, 2017, p. 11). In Extra-Dependent Teams, competition leads to the superior practice of elders and Core members not being shared with newcomers because of the immediate loss that such an act would have to their competitive advantage within the team. At the same time team members spend more time fighting for minimal targets, arguing about the latest reward mechanism or conspiring to manipulate the figures so that they deliver their target, irrespective of what other damage it creates elsewhere in the team or the organisation (and note, these are their dependents). For newcomers surrounded by knowledgeable peers who desert them in their time of need, the easiest choice is to get whatever they can from the experience before leaving for grass that is greener. It means many of the team never quite get the full repertoire of the common practice which leaves a minority of team members to deliver an imbalanced and bare minimum combined capability.

Ironically, this approach is self-perpetuating as the 'best' practitioner typically becomes the next line manager (or leaves to line manage a similar team elsewhere) and uses the logic of 'what got me here must be good, because I came out on top'. They consequently re-use the approach, keeping it breathing, but not more bountiful.

Collaboration

The other best guess approach is the complete opposite – collaboration. Helping each other out is a positive act of kindness which is hard to reproach; indeed, it is something to encourage. But in Extra-Dependent Teams this offer of help is easily taken as direct support through working together. Because team members in Extra-Dependent Teams depend on people outside the team to deliver their performance rather than people inside the team, working together inevitably means putting more effort in than is required to get the job done. The easiest similarity is when you walk into a shop and there are two people on one checkout. Checkouts are designed for one person, so two people is overcapacity. Indeed, two people on the checkout would not only be inefficient, it would cause ineffectiveness as two sets of hands scanning the customer's shopping will *slow* the process down rather than speed it up. Even if the customer has a particularly large shopping bag, it makes no sense to have two people operate the checkout – it's still only a one-person job.

The Team School is correct in seeing the limitations of collaboration for the sake of it. The key to collaboration is understanding when, where, how and why people can collaborate for mutual benefit. If we take the same scenario, two people at a checkout, it makes sense if one is *teaching* the other how to run the process. This is much more akin to Extra-Dependent Teams where newcomers learn from existing members. The balancing act for the teacher is collaborating, not for the sake of it, but for a quick transfer to *independence*. The more the teacher works alongside the newcomer, the less effective they are together. The reverse is also true: the less time the teacher spends bringing the newcomer up to the agreed standard of the shared repertoire, the more effective both team members can be when they return to working separately. Ironically, many 'team players' are seen to be the people who spend *more* time rather than less time with colleagues. As we will see in Chapter 8, Extra-Dependent Team development, the art of development is getting the most out of the minimum time together and not simply working together for the sake of it.

Management by exception

All too often, after a manager has tried collaboration and competitiveness and has found neither to be worth the effort, they adopt a completely hands-off approach, only stepping in when something goes wrong – when there is an exception to the expected standard. It means the manager predominantly leaves the team members alone to get on with things. They might only get involved if targets are at risk, standards are noticeably dropped or complaints are made. This approach is fairly normal in organisations for a number of reasons: it's an easy option for managers to adopt whilst still being seen to 'manage'; it can sometimes be popular with team members because it keeps the line manager 'off my back'; and it can therefore also be (mis)understood to be 'empowering' and 'trusting' of team members to get on with their work without constant supervision. In reality, it's a mutually acceptable stand-off. As one member of an Extra-Dependent Team in a global IT company once told me, 'I'm happy because my manager leaves me alone and he's happy because I don't cause him any more work'. But what value beyond $1 + 1 = 2$ is being gained from such a relationship? Clearly none.

Sometimes the team members expect more from their managers; they aren't happy with this 'stand-off' with their line manager because they expect more.

For instance, another person I spoke with who also worked in an Extra-Dependent Team but in a completely different global IT organisation said that his day-to-day Inter-Dependent Team that he worked in performed really well and was successful. But when asked to describe what it was like in his Extra-Dependent Team he said, 'it sucks' because the team rarely met and he hardly saw his boss apart from the obligatory monthly one to ones.

Yet there can be so much value shared across Extra-Dependent Teams. They can be places to flourish together. But it takes proactive management, not reactive management, do to that. We therefore move onto our level 2 mental model, teams or groups.

Team OR group management

In this level of mental model the manager's options are channelled into two camps – actions associated with creating a team or actions associated with managing a group.

Team

We have already looked at many of the reasons why a manager of an Extra-Dependent Team may decide to manage his team in accordance with the conventional mental model of teams:

- Lots of examples of Inter-Dependent Teams are readily available – sports teams, etc. – to provide inspiration and an example of how to do it.
- The team doesn't act in the way that is intended and therefore it looks dysfunctional (herding cats).
- Pressure from senior managers to develop.
- HR experts provide a template to follow which matches the conventional model.
- A desire to achieve the promise of synergy.
- A desire to be seen to do the right thing.

Any one of these is sufficient cause to attempt to manage an Extra-Dependent Team in an inter-dependent way. However, such an approach can cause problems. Here are a few examples.

Setting the team up for failure

Trying to develop the team can make things worse. Let us return to the IT team of which the member said 'it sucks'. It was a team of product managers who all managed different products and worked with different people around the world to develop, sell and bill that product. They were a typical Extra-Dependent Team.

The line manager wanted to do more than just 'best guess' management. Like many aspiring managers, she decided that she wanted to manage a team, not a group. So the manager arranged for the team to do some team-building activities. The main activity of the day was to build and fire a catapult – a task requiring the team to work together to achieve a common goal. It would also be fun. Unfortunately, the day ended with neither being achieved.

The trouble was that the product managers never worked together in the conventional mental model sense. They only reported to the same line manager. So doing an activity like building a catapult was only ever going to be a one-off. To build a catapult you need to work as an Inter-Dependent Team, not an Extra-Dependent Team. And because they were all product managers, they didn't have the range of different skills necessary to work interdependently – they were too similar. So when it came to building a catapult, they failed to work together cohesively and they didn't achieve the common goal. During a review of the activity the manager left the team in no doubt that the failure to build a catapult reflected their lack of cohesion and team spiritedness. If the team had any team spirit before this event, it had none after it. The manager had completely misread the team.

In fact, each of the team members was a very capable and loyal Inter-Dependent Team member – just not to this product management team. Instead, they applied their capability to those they worked with to see their products sell successfully. The manager would have had a much better result getting these informal Inter-Dependent Teams to build a catapult rather than the product manager team. But then, ironically, she wouldn't have needed to do so, because they already worked well together.

Ineffective team meetings

But it's not just team-building events that can become problematic in an Extra-Dependent Team. Regular team meetings for Extra-Dependent Teams can be ineffective if they are run as if the team is inter-dependent. Let's return to Erik's engineering team. I attended one of Erik's regular Monday morning meetings for his engineering team to observe what went on. The routine agenda of the team meeting consisted of sharing with each other what each team member was doing, what priorities they had during that week and what help they might need. The manager went around the table giving each team member time to speak.

During this meeting the engineering manager worked incredibly hard – listening intently and offering comment – which was in contrast to the team members who sat still and only spoke when it was their turn. To the engineering manager this was very frustrating. But it was equally frustrating for the team members as what they did and what priority they gave it were their individual responsibilities and no one else in the team was materially affected. Why wait for Monday morning, when all these things can be done via email in a manner more suited to the needs of the work? What is the point in all getting together for a meeting when no one else is really affected by what I'm doing anyway? By running meetings in this way, it makes the team appear dysfunctional, when actually the team is *entirely* functional without the meeting. If team meetings focused instead on developing the common practice then the team would have a reason to meet.

Creating difference rather than similarity

With the conventional mental model an Extra-Dependent Team manager will tend towards identifying different strengths within the team in order to deliver better performance. Before I started to work with Malinda and her risk team, Malinda had already arranged the team around their different strengths putting different regional risk managers in charge of developing competencies and standards in areas that reflected their individual strengths. There is nothing wrong with this per se, but it had allowed the team to think it operated as an Inter-Dependent Team, where they could expect to rely on each other's strengths. Such an approach left one regional risk manager thinking he was going to specialise in supporting financial risk management whilst another would specialise in assessment and management of scheduling risk, and another focusing on planning value-management activities each to suit their strengths. Yet because each regional risk manager was individually accountable for their own separate region, none was in a position to provide their specialism to others outside their region.

When I suggested to Malinda that each region really expected their respective regional risk manager to be competent in all areas of risk rather than just some as the team had been requesting, it came both as a surprise and as completely obvious to him. Yet such a suggestion countered the conventional mental model of teams. One team member challenged, 'If we're a team, aren't we supposed to work to our strengths?' when presented with the expectation that he was supposed to be able to do everything reasonably well, rather than something really well and other things not so well. The requirement of the organisation and the structure that the team was working to meant that they couldn't be a team reliant on each other's strengths – they had to be consistently strong in all areas. If the team had continued to work to their strengths in line with the conventional mental model of teams, then there was a high risk that the team would fail across all regions, unable to offer the full repertoire expected to deliver combined capability.

Group

On the face of it, out of all of the approaches described so far, treating an Extra-Dependent Team as if it were just a group is possibly the closest match for what it is. By considering direct reports as forming a group rather than a team, the manager may at least acknowledge that their 'team' doesn't match the conventional mental model and therefore they might decide to manage things differently. I did have the pleasure of working with a senior HR manager who had decided to manage her team of HR business partners in a way that matched the Extra-Dependent Team approach outlined in subsequent chapters. So there will no doubt be managers in organisations trying to find a realistic and relevant approach to managing Extra-Dependent Teams, having never heard the term and realising that the conventional model was inappropriate.

Notwithstanding the odd example, as identified above, the typical approach to managing a group is by focusing on achieving at the very least the sum of the parts. The manager's responsibility is to ensure that each part delivers what is expected. The manager focuses on three areas: job allocation, to ensure that people match the work; continuity, to ensure that should anything happen to the team member, someone else in the team can pick up the work; and keeping everyone happy – because a happy team takes less maintenance than a frustrated team.

An example of how this is expressed by a manager came during a team event I ran with an Extra-Dependent Team of project managers. The project managers acknowledged that everyone in the team needed to be consistent and saw the merit of sharing best practice together. However, the manager's reasons for consistency were revealed when she suddenly said, 'It's all about what to do if you're eaten by a tiger!' At first I didn't quite understand what she meant and was sure that many of the project managers weren't clear either, so I asked her to explain. She said that should any of the team be eaten by a tiger, then consistency across the team would ensure that someone was on hand to take their place. Consistency for the manager was about the ability to guarantee continuity of service, her ability to allocate the jobs. She didn't really have the team members' interests or aspirations at heart.

Of course, with a focus like that, it can appear the manager doesn't care and leads to people seeking opportunities elsewhere. Ironically, this creates the continuity issue the manager is so fearful of.

Inter-Dependent Team AND Extra-Dependent Team

So what is involved in managing an Extra-Dependent Team? Let us return to the challenges listed at the beginning of this chapter and address each in turn.

It's not like managing an Inter-Dependent Team

Managing an Extra-Dependent Team is not like managing an Inter-Dependent Team. The power that binds the team together needs to be understood and harnessed, not denied and fought against. In Extra-Dependent Teams an individual's strengths are to be identified so that they can be *shared* amongst the team. Where difference is sought in Inter-Dependent Teams so that people can work together, in Extra-Dependent Teams difference is shared to achieve consistency so that everyone can work better apart.

Team meetings are not a time to hold the team accountable because such public discussions only incite competitiveness between team members or against the manager themselves by way of self-defence. Neither are meetings opportunities to coordinate activity between team members because such coordination activity is much more timely when done via email individually. Instead, team meetings are *opportunities to learn* the shared repertoire from each other so that when they leave the meeting they are more capable in their practice than when they entered.

Conversely, one-to-one meetings are the time to monitor individual accountability. By taking away the public gaze of colleagues, such one-to-one conversations are more likely to be conducted in an open and honest way, addressing reasons for performance being strong or weak. Such performance conversations with all team members provides the manager with an insight into inconsistencies in the shared repertoire. They can then address this through the sharing of strengths in team meetings prompting the team to learn better together.

The accountability is disproportionately borne on the shoulders of the manager

Managing an Extra-Dependent Team in this way provides the team manager with the degree of influence they need to help offset the disproportionate accountability that is borne on their shoulders. The Extra-Dependent Team manager is the sole person responsible for achieving the targets expected of the whole team. It is not a mutually accountable effort. It is the team manager's responsibility therefore to ensure that the team's combined capability matches that target. This is initially done by delegating comparable goals to each individual in the team. This could be a proportion of an overall target or it could be a geographical split of the whole area the manager is responsible for. But having done that, the team is no longer mutually accountable – they are individually accountable. The manager's challenge is to maintain influence over what each individual does because the manager depends on that individual to succeed – even though no one else in the team depends on them. By managing an Extra-Dependent Team in the ways listed above (and developed in subsequent chapters), the manager attains the influence they need to overcome the challenges presented by their disproportionate responsibility.

Empowerment is not a choice, it's a necessity

Influence, however, does not mean control. Because team members in Extra-Dependent Teams work with people outside the team, the notion of empowerment is not optional, it is a necessity. Everyone needs to get on with their own work on their own. They need to be accountable for their own performance and find their own ways of solving the problems they are presented with day in, day out. But this does not mean that an Extra-Dependent Team manager can't provide support. The challenge for the line manager is to provide support in a way that maintains the accountability of the individual and helps them to overcome their own problems, yet without making them feel isolated. To do this, the manager needs to be able to coach.

Coaching is a skill that is increasingly seen as core to the world of managers (Landsberg, 2002; Goleman et al., 2002; Kouzes and Posner, 2007; Whitmore, 2009) because it is a technique that provides tangible support that keeps responsibility and accountability with the person being coached. It therefore helps people make decisions for themselves, inspiring thoughtful action to address meaningful issues that each individual is best placed to deal with. It is similar to the notion described by Haslam et al. as power *through* rather than power *over* others (Haslam et al., 2011, p. 62). There are plenty of other books available to better understand the nuances of coaching so I won't spend much time on it here. But what is particularly important for managers of Extra-Dependent Teams is appreciating that coaching is about, 'unlocking people's potential to maximise their own performance' (Whitmore, 2009, p. 10). The skills of coaching therefore enable the Extra-Dependent Team manager to facilitate learning individually and collectively.

The manager is often also a practitioner

Many Extra-Dependent Teams require the manager to do some of the work themselves – in sporting parlance they are a 'player/manager'. This position of experience makes coaching others particularly challenging for Extra-Dependent Team managers as they could unwittingly believe that they are the experts in the shared repertoire when, in actual fact, others are more capable. Using the three layers, I consider below a number of different scenarios relating to the challenges that a player/manager might find themselves in.

Scenario 1: manager as 'expert'

This situation may look simple because the team member (T) is learning from the manager (M) who is in the Core layer (Figure 6.1). But the challenge for the manager is to avoid a relationship where the experienced manager makes the decisions, leaving the team member less responsible than they need to be for what they are accountable for. In such a situation, the manager needs to use all their coaching ability to support the team member, and not overwhelm them.

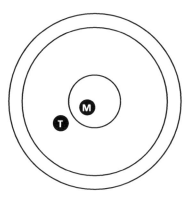

Figure 6.1 Manager as expert.

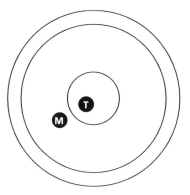

Figure 6.2 Team member as expert.

Scenario 2: team member as 'expert'

This reverse position can be just as challenging for the manager – how can the less experienced manager coach the more experienced team member? Coaching can do this because it facilitates individuals to use their own resourcefulness to stimulate learning. But to use the example of Erik the engineering manager, who was in a similar position with Tony, the manager themselves can be susceptible to under-rating their own experience by asking 'permission' of Core members about what to do (Figure 6.2).

Scenario 3: new team manager

In this third scenario the challenge is a new team manager who may have little experience of the common practice and be on the Periphery of the team. A person who is an experienced manager but with no specific experience in the common practice is a good example of this. The challenge here is for the

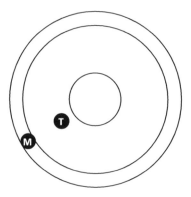

Figure 6.3 New team manager.

manager to be seen to add value to others more experienced than them. In such situations managers need to use their coaching and facilitation skills to enable the team member to learn from themselves and others in the team (Figure 6.3).

Wenger calls this sort of discussion a negotiation of practice because members need to agree what they learn from each other. Whilst negotiating the shared learning can be difficult, it does not have to be. Indeed, several Extra-Dependent Teams I have worked in have been marked by the absence of conflict. But how does conflict happen in Extra-Dependent Teams?

Constructive conflict works differently

Whilst differences of opinion occur, the main issue isn't around the conflict within the team, it is more about the conflict with people outside the team. In essence, each team member is playing a role in at least one other Inter-Dependent Team elsewhere in the organisation. Disagreement is an important part of the Inter-Dependent Team process (Lencioni, 2002) for which the Extra-Dependent Team member is a part. But if they don't associate strongly enough with the Inter-Dependent Team, then they don't conflict constructively, which leads to separation. Commonly the disagreement is seen as an issue between the Extra-Dependent Team and the Inter-Dependent Team and expressed in terms of 'us' and 'them'. An example might be an Extra-Dependent Team member telling their Extra-Dependent Team manager: 'I've told them that we do things in a particular way, but they don't want it done like that. They think they should be treated as a special case. They want things done their way.' The use of 'us' and 'them' is indicative of the distant relationship the Extra-Dependent Team member has with the Inter-Dependent Team in which they work. The challenge for the Extra-Dependent Team manager is to support each team member to be an *active* Inter-Dependent Team player and therefore to *engage in constructive conflict* so that the best outcome can be achieved.

Unfortunately, Extra-Dependent Team managers unconsciously reinforce the 'us' and 'them' of their own team member's position and are not ready enough to coach them to have the difficult conversations that are needed. Such conversations are vital to achieve the performance required. This is an important point which I will expand on in Chapter 7.

The common practice is often influenced by professional bodies remote from the organisation

Finally, because the Extra-Dependent Team is typically part of a wider community of practice of people who undertake similar work in different organisations (sales, risk management, project management, etc.), there is typically a professional body associated with that practice. Such an external professional body can have an indirect influence over the team, something not experienced by Inter-Dependent Teams. New standards, techniques, trending fads, etc. all apply an external pressure onto Extra-Dependent Team managers and force them to make choices: to adapt to the 'industry way' or to adapt to the organisation's way. For instance, whilst Malinda's risk team was developing a unique framework of competencies to meet the needs of the organisation, a peer function of project management was basing all its competencies on the generic professional standards. Both approaches have merit, but the Extra-Dependent Team manager needs to be mindful of whose agenda is being pursued – the team's, the organisation's or the profession's.

The shared repertoire of the Extra-Dependent Team manager

So what does it take to be a manager of an Extra-Dependent Team? What is the shared repertoire of an Extra-Dependent Team manager? Below are some of the skills, behaviours, activities and resources that might be expected. It will not be exhaustive and neither will it be permanent. As the practice of Extra-Dependent Team management develops, so will the shared repertoire.

Skills

Skills and behaviours with self

- Self-awareness – the ability to be able to accurately assess their own strengths and weaknesses.
- Desire to learn and to learn *how* to learn – without this the Extra-Dependent Team manager cannot role model what the team does.
- An interest in developing other people – without this the team will be diminished.
- An appetite to operate within the wider organisation and beyond – because this is where the team's performance is experienced.
- Ability to trust themselves – to be self-confident enough to be able to be confident in others.

Skills and behaviours with individuals

- Listening, really listening – without listening the manager cannot understand; understand the meaning someone is trying to convey, not just the words that they say.
- Asking powerful questions – this is the life blood of coaching and facilitating learning in others.
- Coaching – draw out the best in people, appreciating what they can do, rather than what they can't.
- Providing personal feedback – personal feedback isn't the feedback you garner from others and then share as a 'messenger'. This is feedback that comes personally from you and goes personally to them. It makes for a more honest, clean and productive learning process.
- Engage productively in difficult conversations – without this neither the manager, nor team members, nor stakeholders will get a complete understanding of each other at the most difficult of times when it matters most.
- Be able to trust others – they need to make decisions for themselves and the manager needs to trust them to see it through.
- Be able to encourage and support team members in challenging conversations they need to have with others outside the team.

Skills and behaviours with the team

- Be able to facilitate discussions – so that meetings are engaging discussions that stimulate learning.
- Understand and be able to manage group dynamics – respond to what is going on inside and outside the room so that the group dynamics are productive rather than dysfunctional.
- Able to challenge thinking and practice – wherever they are in the layers, the manager needs to be able to address assumptions and restrictive practices.
- Be able to identify with the team and to enable them to identify with the manager – this takes self-disclosure, sharing stories (good and bad) that relate honestly with the common practice so that the team can see the manager as 'one of us'.
- Promote, manage and accomplish continuous change – keep building the common practice so that the combined capability is fully maximised.
- Craft identity – the reputation of the team needs to be carefully crafted from inside and outside the team.

Skills and behaviours with the system

- Understand and engage with organisational dynamics – don't ignore it as office 'politics'; the way the organisation works is directly relevant to the team's shared repertoire, combined capability and reputation.
- Systems thinking – don't think of the organisation as a hierarchy; engage with it as a system involving interdependencies and extra-dependencies

that connect people inside and outside the organisation. Then managers can appreciate the value they create, how and why they create it.

- Be a good networker – to engage with stakeholders willingly and regularly, to keep an ear out for problems, developments and opportunities.
- Think strategically – an Extra-Dependent Team manager has a strategic impact due to the way the team performs through others.
- Keep up to date with professional developments – maintain a watch on developments elsewhere in the practice, but don't subject the team or the organisation to the latest 'fad' if it is inappropriate for the organisation and its customers.

Activities a manager needs to get involved with

- Goal setting – to ensure individuals know what is expected of them.
- Regular one-to-one meetings with the whole team – to monitor performance and to coach.
- Regular team meetings – to learn together, share strengths, solutions, overcome common problems and improve the combined capability.
- Occasional deep-dive team meetings – to break any routine of regular team meetings and be able to critically think about the common practice and the value it provides.
- Meetings with stakeholders – to monitor their use and benefit of the combined capability.
- Administration – to build and reinforce the shared repertoire.
- Networking conversations – to keep abreast of the bigger picture inside and outside the organisation and to craft the team's reputation from the outside.

Resources that need to be managed for the team

- Communication systems – to help coordinate activity, schedule, inform, report.
- IT systems appropriate for running the team within the organisation.
- Processes that record how the work is done.
- Standards that enable team members to appreciate what is expected of them.
- Finance to invest in maintaining or developing the resources.
- Equipment – anything required for the common practice.

What's my team's identity?

As we finish this chapter on Extra-Dependent Team management, it is worth considering how a manager might recognise if they were doing things well or not. One way of doing that, which I have found has helped me, is to map the Extra-Dependent Team dynamics and consider how they reflect the reputation that the team might have. The examples in Table 6.1 are

Table 6.1 Example of identities within Extra-Dependent Teams

Cultivating

Description
Strong repertoire role modelled by several elders.
Newcomers are welcomed quickly on a purposeful
inbound trajectory. Active members challenge existing
ways and are encouraged to do so. Elders have an
appetite for continuous improvement and encourage
ideas and new thinking. Team reputation is strong to
match the combined capability.
Underlying influence
The team is learning well together, using everyone. It
remains dynamic and close to the needs of those people
it depends on.
Management action
Continue to meet, develop, perform, encourage,
challenge and flourish.

Cloven

Description
The identity is split between a dominant elder inner
circle and relatively high turnover of newcomers who
linger for as long as they can on the Periphery before
leaving. Penetrating through Active to the Core is
difficult. Reputation is mixed due to the inconsistent
experience of the combined capability. Elders operate as
an inner clique which risks the long-term sustainability
of the team.
Underlying influence
It might be that elders are not sufficiently welcoming
of newcomers. Alternatively, the team lacks a clear
development programme from newcomer to Core
member.
Management action
Elders to mentor newcomers to develop meaningful and
practical learning pathways towards the core. Monitor
the elders and ensure that the clique is being eroded,
rather than reinforced. Encourage the newcomers to
question the shared repertoire. Ensure that you keep
close to the elders to maintain their trust and respect.

Committee

Description
The identity is inconsistent because with no Core
members, no one really role models the repertoire in a
way that is engaging for others. Each Active member
conducts their work in a different way to other Active
members. Newcomers therefore take a while to progress
to Active member as they are not sure what to learn. Core
membership is resisted as too high profile or too much
work, or denied through unconscious collusion – i.e. 'If I
won't be Core, then no-one will'. Reputation is poor.
Underlying influence
There is a lack of leadership in the common practice.
No one is willing to take the lead. Everyone is happier
to disagree than agree – they see more differences
between each other than similarities.

Management action

Select several Active members to champion as role models. Move them into Core. Coach them on taking a more responsible position as role model – setting an example of how to learn from each other, not that they are the experts for others to comply with. Be careful not to take up the Core position yourself, unless you are accompanied by others – see Cult below.

Cult

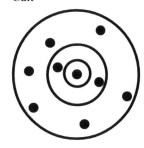

Description

The identity is centred around one dominant elder in the Core supported by protective 'disciples' in the Active layer. Other members find it hard to advance beyond the periphery, never quite being 'good enough' and always overshadowed by the dominant elder. Identity of team exists by association to single elder. Reputation is dominated by the elder – for better or worse.

Underlying influence

The dominant elder wishes to retain control over the shared repertoire. There are principally two motivations for the elder to do this. Firstly, to maintain a superior position as a way of retaining vestiges of control over the performance of the team. Secondly, it may be that the elder is fundamentally shifting the common practice leaving everyone else significantly out of step with them and finding it difficult to keep up.

Management action

This is tricky because the dominant elder is likely to be the manager! If so, then the first motivation above will be difficult to overcome without going through a significant personal development first – or leaving the team. If it is the second motivation, then do more to address the disciples – coach them into a core position, or recruit peripheral members into the active layer to weaken the defensive stance of the disciples. Get these active members to connect you to the periphery more – so that the team can become more cohesive.

Coven

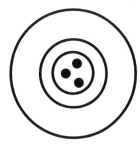

Description

The identity is exclusive and remote. Boundaries are repelling and no one has a way of getting in – or out. Reputation is very strong but perhaps not always positive or progressive. The combined capability might not meet the volumes required.

Underlying influence

A few elders tightly control the common practice. They believe that they are the only people who can do it, or they believe that newcomers would render them redundant. They therefore cling to a very tight identity (falsely) secure in the knowledge that they are the only people who could possibly do this work.

(*Continued*)

Table 6.1 (Continued)

Management action
Take action fast. Recruit people into the team (numerically more than the elders if you can) to break things up, or consider starting afresh. Understand the needs of the stakeholders and use this to articulate a vision for the practice and the future team's reputation.

hypothesised, but I have subsequently experienced several of these in real Extra-Dependent Teams and having these examples helped me as a consultant and as a manager to adjust my actions to address underlying issues.

References

Chartered Management Institute (2017) Chartered manager, Managers.org.uk, 29 November, www.managers.org.uk/employers/management-training-our-services/~/media/Angela-Media-Library/pdfs/Chartered%20Manager/Chartered%20 Manager%20-%20General

Goleman, D, Boyatzis, R and McKee, A (2002) *The New Leaders: Transforming the Art of Leadership into the Science of Results*, Little, Brown, London.

Haslam, S A, Reicher, S D and Platow, M J (2011) *The New Psychology of Leadership: Identity, Influence and Power*, Psychology Press, Hove.

Kouzes, J M and Posner, B Z (2007) *The Leadership Challenge*, 4th Ed., Jossey-Bass, San Francisco.

Landsberg, M (2002) *The Tao of Coaching*, Profile Books, London.

Lencioni, P (2002) *The Five Dysfunctions of a Team*, Jossey-Bass, San Francisco.

Whitmore, J (2009) *Coaching for Performance: GROWing Human Potential and Purpose: The Principles and Practice of Coaching and Leadership*, 4th Ed., Nicholas Brealey, London.

7 Extra-Dependent Team performance

The promise of synergy is the driving force behind promoting teams within organisations. Synergy is the way that a team bonds together to achieve more than the sum of its individual parts. For organisations that are expected to deliver 'more for less', synergy provides the answer.

But synergy is not just the total output of a group of people. The value of teams runs much deeper, such as having a sense of belonging, building a sense of identity and generating meaning in one's life. When people have these things, they are stronger in themselves, more resilient and less likely to be stressed. A strong sense of belonging is even shown to help with mental health issues (Haslam, 2014).

Organisations exist in order to *do* something for others elsewhere in the wider system and teams are formed in organisations in order for people to play their part and add value to what that something is. When teams play their part well, their results help members feel good about what they do and so they continue to find ways to play a valuable part. It's a virtuous cycle where wellbeing is generated from good performance and good performance is generated from wellbeing. As General Stanley McChrystal explains in his book *Team of Teams*: 'Studies at large companies with robust data sets such as Xerox, Ford, and P&G have found that the implementation of teams often leads to leaps in productivity as well as improvements in morale' (McChrystal et al., 2015, p. 125).

Synergy is therefore a combination of both productivity and wellbeing. I have often heard the saying that 'we are not human *doings*, we are human *beings*', where the point being made is that we do too much and miss the point in life – who we are. To some extent I agree with this. Yet what I have described so far in this book, building on the great work of the Team School and Community of Practice School, *doing* is directly connected with *being*. Being is about who we are and who we are is shaped by what we do. Performance in teams is therefore about achieving meaningful output – for others and ourselves.

Performance within complexity

Achieving synergy with others is difficult within complex organisations where employees can be in multiple teams simultaneously. The aim of meaningful output can be easily lost within the confusion of matrix management and constant change. In such environments, teams become even more important as reliable places to belong and flourish. Yet if all managers followed the same model of teams then employees spanning multiple teams concurrently are pulled in different directions. It's possible to do, but in practical terms employees are required to prioritise one team over the other.

In my work with organisations I experience two versions of this prioritisation. Firstly, team members explain their relationship with multiple teams as having a 'solid line to [this team] and a dotted line to [this team]' as if this was in some way an explanation of the different relationships between each team. When I ask people to explain the difference more specifically, their answer typically demonstrates that they have not clarified that difference for themselves. More accurately, 'lines' are used to justify prioritisation of one manager over another. The 'solid line' manager is expected to hold them accountable for their performance and so is given priority. The 'dotted line' manager on the other hand too often de-prioritises responsibility for the team member's performance, sometimes to the point of abdication, thinking that they don't have the 'authority' to deal with it. This triangular issue, involving the team member and their two respective managers, is at the heart of how to manage performance in an Extra-Dependent Team, as I will outline below.

Secondly, I also hear managers, consultants and even team coaches *insisting* that people prioritise one team over another – indeed, I've been tempted to do so myself. In each case, the person believes that their target team is the priority team. But it is simply a way of claiming power; it's a selfish act that doesn't appreciate the needs of others within the complexity of the system – and can distort the way that people need to work together to enable the organisation to perform. So whilst performance is addressed within the priority team other areas of performance are likely to be neglected. It is analogous to seeing the lungs as less important than the heart within the body. But without the lungs, there is no oxygen in the blood for the heart to pump around the body. Complex organisations, just like bodies, need every part to be performing or else everything suffers. So managing performance is key to keeping the organisation alive.

Conventional mental model of teams and performance management

The act of managing performance is dominated by the process of managers setting goals for their reports and then appraising them of how well they are doing (Chartered Institute of Personnel and Development, 2016). Whatever the process is in whatever organisation, the individual experience of a team member is dominated by the interaction they have with their line manager.

As Marcus Buckingham highlights the manager is the most important person in the process:

> She defines and pervades your work environment. If she sets clear expectations, knows you, trusts you, and invests in you, then you can forgive the company its lack of a profit-sharing program. But if your relationship with your manager is fractured, then no amount of in-chair massaging or company-sponsored dog walking will persuade you to stay and perform.
>
> (Buckingham and Coffman, 2005, p. 28)

The performance-management process is down to the quality of the relationship between the manager and the direct report. Because Extra-Dependent Team members work with people outside the team, the team manager often isn't in a position to define and pervade the work environment as Buckingham expects. Indeed, they can often be very remote from it. Yet the performance-management process requires them to appraise performance in a knowledgeable way, a trusting way, a fair way – otherwise the relationship with the manager becomes fractured. Given the realities of how Extra-Dependent Teams are structured, coupled with the orthodox process of performance management, it appears that Extra-Dependent Team managers are being set up to fail.

Let me illustrate this with a fairly typical performance-management process in an Extra-Dependent Team:

1. A member of an Extra-Dependent team works hard with other people outside the team to deliver what is expected. They do the best they can, using their current capability to deliver what they are asked.
2. Throughout this process the Extra-Dependent Team manager doesn't witness what goes on because they are not involved in the work. But the Inter-Dependent Team manager does experience the person's work.
3. The orthodox performance-management process requires the direct line manager to manage performance. So the Extra-Dependent Team manager holds monthly one-to-one 'catch-ups' with the team member in order to discuss issues or problems they might be having. During these conversations the Extra-Dependent Team manager provides whatever support and guidance that they can (coaching is important here, but more of that later). But they find it hard because they are unable to verify the team member's account of what goes well and what goes badly. Clearly, the team member is only telling their side of the story. So the line manager approaches other people who work with the team member – specifically targeting the Inter-Dependent Team manager.
4. The Extra-Dependent Team manager asks the Inter-Dependent Team manager for feedback on how the team member is getting on. What do

they find they do well? What could they improve on? It's all textbook questions to support the team member in understanding their contribution, whilst also helping them identify ways to improve.

5   Having got this feedback from the Inter-Dependent Team manager, the Extra-Dependent Team manager then shares it with the team member in the next catch-up.

6   During the conversation the feedback shared to the team member doesn't quite stack up. The team member thinks that their contribution isn't being acknowledged and therefore not sufficiently valued. The team member tries to explain their perspective again, but the more they do, the more defensive they become. The manager in response only has the Inter-Dependent Team manager's version to fall back on and can only speculate as to how to interpret it.

7   Very quickly the trust between line manager and direct report starts to wane and the manager, who needs to make an assessment, has three no-win options:

   a   Continue to gather more evidence to validate the report's evidence, but by doing so, undermining the trust they have from their direct report.
   b   Come down on the side of trust and take the direct report's evidence on balance, but in so doing undermining the trust they have with important stakeholders of the team.
   c   Avoid making a decision at all by averaging out the evidence, but by doing so taking all meaning from the performance-management process and undermining one of the key roles in line management.

What is intended to be a constructive and fulfilling conversation turns into a process at high risk of generating disengagement. What makes it worse is that all the Inter-Dependent Team managers in the organisation don't take issue with this process because it works for them and their direct reports. This leads everyone to think that it isn't the process that's broken – it's the Extra-Dependent Team manager.

I believe that this situation is commonplace in organisations. Every day Extra-Dependent Team managers are trying to manage performance in a way that is not fit for purpose, and by doing so they are constantly at risk of fracturing their relationship with their direct reports – the one relationship that they need to be open, honest, trustworthy and fair.

So how should performance management be conducted in an Extra-Dependent Team? Clearly it needs to be meaningful for the team member and, since they work with others outside the team, it needs to involve them as well. But it needs to be authentic and genuine and for this it needs to recognise which manager does what: what is the part played by a 'solid line' manager and what part is played by a 'dotted line' manager when it comes to performance? I believe this leads to a different approach to managing performance which engages all three key parties meaningfully.

Overcoming the performance challenge

Firstly, each manager has a different performance responsibility:

Extra-Dependent Team manager	Responsible for developing the best possible *capability* in a specific practice that is then used by Inter-Dependent Teams.
Inter-Dependent Team manager	Responsible for achieving the best possible *objectives* through using a mix of specific capabilities.

By recognising this distinction it means Inter-Dependent Team managers can expect their 'dotted line' members from Extra-Dependent Teams to play a meaningful part in the process of delivering performance towards their common goal. Similarly, Extra-Dependent Team managers can expect their team members' contribution in an Inter-Dependent Team to be handled directly by Inter-Dependent Team managers. The focus of performance management in Extra-Dependent Teams therefore is around each team member adopting and adapting the shared repertoire to maximise the combined capability that they can deliver into Inter-Dependent Teams. When both managers know they are doing something different, both can ensure they play complementary roles for the individual – not competitive roles. So rather than pulling the organisation apart, all three glue it together.

Consider Figure 7.1. The generic Inter-Dependent Team led by manager D is made up of a number of complementary capabilities (C, E and F) with specialist B capability coming from a peer Extra-Dependent Team. On the organogram it is indicated by the classic 'solid' and 'dotted' lines. The Extra-Dependent Team made up of Bs has the job of providing maximum combined capability through an individual specialist B. In turn, the Inter-Dependent Team depends on that specialist B capability to achieve the team's common goal.

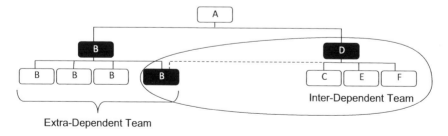

Figure 7.1 The positioning of people responsible for managing performance.

We therefore have a situation where three specific people have a responsibility for managing performance:

Inter-Dependent Team *manager* D – Responsible for ensuring everyone in the Inter-Dependent Team works together as a team, combining their complementary capabilities to achieve a common goal. The whole team needs to consider themselves mutually accountable for achieving (or not achieving) the common goal.
Extra-Dependent Team *manager* B – Responsible for maximising the combined capability available through Extra-Dependent Team member B and also ensuring that this combined capability is being used correctly, to the required standards within the team managed by Inter-Dependent Team manager D.
Extra-Dependent Team *member* B – Responsible for applying the combined capability of B in support of the Inter-Dependent Team's common goal. They need to work with everyone in the Inter-Dependent Team, even if this proves difficult, in order to deliver their part in the team's performance.

In practice, this means an Extra-Dependent Team manager can manage performance through prompting three different conversations involving different combinations of each of these people. It is called the performance triangle.

The Extra-Dependent Team performance triangle

Each of the following conversations needs to be had to ensure performance (Figure 7.2).

Conversation 1: Extra-Dependent Team manager with team member

In this conversation the Extra-Dependent Team manager needs to focus on two aspects of performance: the individuals' ability to deliver their combined

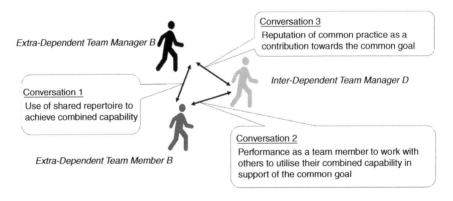

Figure 7.2 The performance management triangle.

capability to the Inter-Dependent Team at the appropriate standard and the individuals' learning that allows them to maximise the combined capability within the Extra-Dependent Team. The conversation needs to focus on what aspects of the combined capability are being used in the work they do outside the team. The performance conversation will need to revolve around the individuals' goal progress, standards of application, appropriateness of application and also monitor what they are doing to adapt the shared repertoire to suit the local requirements of the Inter-Dependent Team.

But the conversation also needs to explore the shared repertoire, where they are strong in it and where they are weak, what they are learning and what they can offer. It needs to explore how they are contributing to the continuous improvement of the shared repertoire and what part the individual might play in that, especially with regards to sharing their good practice with others in the team – for instance, if they were an elder or Core member.

On the other side of the conversation, the Extra-Dependent Team member is accountable for achieving their individual goals with regards to the work they do. These goals might be around utilisation by Inter-Dependent Teams, the amount of specialist work they do for others outside the team, or it might be around a specific key performance indicator, such as a sales target. But team members, even newcomers or elders, also need to be responsible for sharing what they do best with others in the team and identifying where they need to learn from others in order to improve their shared repertoire.

Throughout this conversation the Extra-Dependent Team manager needs to adopt a coaching style in order to foster a learning relationship with the team member and to encourage them to be accountable for themselves. This learning relationship is important so that the team member feels safe enough to highlight mistakes or to seek help from others in the team. Because they have similar conversations with everyone in the team, the manager has a view across the team of the current state of the shared repertoire.

The coaching style also allows the Extra-Dependent Team manager to have a meaningful conversation with the team member about issues they have with the work they do in the Inter-Dependent Teams, without undermining the relationship. The team member may for instance experience problems implementing the shared repertoire in the desired way. Through coaching, the manager can prompt the exploration of these issues and potential ways of adapting the shared repertoire to address local issues.

For the Extra-Dependent Team manager, the toughest part of this conversation is around encouraging the team member to *work together better* with the Inter-Dependent Team. This means coaching them around how to engage with the team, what responsibility they have to the Inter-Dependent Team manager and how to work through areas of potential conflict with other people in that team. This is important because the Extra-Dependent Team member needs to be ready to have an open and honest performance conversation with the Inter-Dependent Team manager.

Conversation 2: Inter-Dependent Team manager with team member

Irrespective of whether this relationship is a 'solid line' or 'dotted line' on an organogram, this performance conversation needs to happen. Without it, not everyone in the Inter-Dependent Team is held mutually accountable for achieving the common goal. Because the performance of the team partly depends on the specialist capability that the Extra-Dependent Team member provides, the performance conversation is entirely legitimate when it covers areas such as how they work with others in the team, how that work is progressing, at what rate and in which direction. It might also involve how flexible they are to others' requirements on the team, how they support or engage with others and how they hold each other to account.

Of course, all these aspects are exactly the sort of things that the Team School promotes as good practice in Inter-Dependent Teams. The important difference here is that the Extra-Dependent Team member acknowledges that they are an active and legitimate member of that Inter-Dependent Team, even though they have a different line manager, and that the Inter-Dependent Team manager is right to have the performance conversations with them about how to work with others on the team to achieve the common goal.

Even though I have presented this performance conversation as one to one, in practical terms and in accordance to the approach of the Team School it is likely to be a whole-team conversation in keeping with the mutual accountability required of Inter-Dependent Teams. It means that Extra-Dependent Team members will need to attend Inter-Dependent Team meetings in order to account for themselves, to challenge others and to develop new ways of working so that they all succeed together.

There is a third conversation that also needs to happen – between the two managers themselves.

Conversation 3: Extra-Dependent Team manager with
Inter-Dependent Team manager

The challenge with only having the first two conversations is that:

- The responsibility is with the team member to make it all work.
- It distances the Extra-Dependent Team manager from those who value the combined capability.
- There is a lack of understanding by either manager about what might be possible or indeed expected of the team member.

Yet, as I have already illustrated, this third conversation typically goes wrong because it focuses on a performance assessment of the individual concerned. Of all the Extra-Dependent Teams that I have worked with, studied or developed, not one has previously recognised manager-to-manager conversations as anything more than appraisal feedback. Yet there is a legitimate conversation to be had between both managers about what common practice is being offered (by the Extra-Dependent Team manager) and how it is being used effectively (by the Inter-Dependent Team manager). It makes it a performance-management conversation between peers about what each is responsible for achieving – not what the team member is achieving.

For the Extra-Dependent Team manager, this conversation allows them to appreciate how the Inter-Dependent Team manager is viewing the combined capability that is on offer. Remember this is about the full shared repertoire of the team – their processes, IT systems, equipment, skills, etc.:

- Is the Inter-Dependent Team manager using it as much as they could?
- Are they aware of the latest developments that the team is learning to use?
- What standard is the Inter-Dependent Team manager expecting of the capability?
- What are they actually getting?
- Is it enough for their purposes?
- What would happen if it was twice as much or half as much?
- What capability might be missing?

The conversation is not about the individual team member. Instead, it is around identifying and addressing performance gaps in the nature of the combined capability as well as the way that this is being used to maximise the value of the Inter-Dependent Team's common goal.

It also provides the opportunity for the Extra-Dependent Team manager to develop the reputation of the team. This is not about some gimmicky promotion of the team, it's about ensuring that the combined capability being offered is making the difference within the Inter-Dependent Team that is intended. For instance, in Erik's engineering team discussed in Chapter 5, Erik was aware that Sally was not only a good engineer, but was also able to support less experienced project managers to run their projects. This was very generous of both Sally and Erik and it seemed to work. But Erik was also aware that it shouldn't overstep the mark. If Sally started to do too much support for the project manager, then there was a risk that the engineering capability would deteriorate. If this happened, then it would not only affect Sally's and Erik's ability to deliver what they were each accountable for, it would also reflect the team's reputation for providing dependable engineering capability. So these manager-to-manager performance conversations are opportunities to ensure that each manager is playing their part in using the combined capability appropriately.

Given the tradition of feedback the Extra-Dependent Team manager should anticipate the Inter-Dependent Team manager will want to provide feedback about the team member. Where this is intended to address underperformance with the team member, the Extra-Dependent Team manager needs to be ready to ensure they don't take on a responsibility best held by the Inter-Dependent Team manager. For instance, if the Inter-Dependent Team manager is unhappy that the team member turns up late to his or her meetings, it is entirely right for that to be addressed by the Inter-Dependent Team manager themselves. The most direct and honest conversation to address an issue like that is between the Inter-Dependent Team manager and the Extra-Dependent Team member because it is about how they work together with the rest of the Inter-Dependent Team. Doing it any other way is ducking responsibility and complicating matters. It is avoiding the difficult conversations that need to happen in Inter-Dependent Teams in order for them to work well together and achieve the common goal. Channelling such a conversation through the Extra-Dependent Team manager is *not* holding the Inter-Dependent Team mutually accountable. So the Extra-Dependent Team manager needs to decline to request to pass this feedback on and urge the Inter-Dependent Team manager to do it – as in Conversation 2.

On the other hand, if the conversation between the two managers highlights that the team member doesn't have enough time to come to the team meetings, then this is a common practice issue and therefore something that the Extra-Dependent Team manager *does* take responsibility for. For instance, perhaps the team member is overstretched? Perhaps the Inter-Dependent Team manager is expecting more of their time than had been previously agreed? Perhaps there is a change in the pace of the Inter-Dependent Team that requires a greater combined capability than the team member can provide on their own? These are areas for the Extra-Dependent Team manager to deal with – to improve flexibility of the combined capability, to manage fluctuations in capacity, to renegotiate how much of the combined capability is needed by the Inter-Dependent Team. This third performance conversation between managers is therefore really important to address performance at a higher level within the organisation. We will also see in Chapter 8 that this conversation is vital for developing the strategic impact of the team within the wider organisation.

The performance triangle therefore covers complementary areas within the matrix structure. It means that team members with multiple managers in the matrix are given clear and complementary support by those different managers. For the team managers it means they play an authentic part in the performance of their respective teams, but as part of the wider organisation. For the team member the two separate performance conversations enable them to achieve things that aren't possible through a single line manager conversation, namely:

- a comprehensive understanding of what is expected of them, both professionally and practically;
- a clear and meaningful assessment of their full value to the organisation from the key people who experience that;
- the ability to give and receive feedback directly and transparently with whom they mutually depend;

- the ability to appreciate their professional strengths and weaknesses by people who understand what they ought to be able to do and also by the people who experience what they are actually able to do;
- be able to raise their awareness of who they can learn from in order to develop their capability further;
- feel unique;
- feel like they matter;
- feel part of a team.

Once we master the dynamics, management and performance of Extra-Dependent Teams then we can start to pursue the elusive status of 'high performance'. For that we need to appreciate how Extra-Dependent Teams develop.

References

Buckingham, M and Coffman, C (2005) *First, Break All the Rules: What the World's Greatest Managers Do Differently*, Pocket Books, London.

Chartered Institute of Personnel and Development (2016) *Could Do Better? Assessing What Works in Performance Management*, Chartered Institute of Personnel and Development, London.

Haslam, P A (2014). Social Identity and the new Psychology of Mental Health. British Psychological Society, Division of Clinical Psychology, Annual Conference, Key Note Speech, Glasgow, 3 December, www.youtube.com/watch?v=TWWZd8lr raw. Accessed on 30th November 2017. Retrieved from www.youtube.com/watch?v= TWWZd8lrraw

McChrystal, G, Collins, T, Silverman, D and Fussell, C (2015) *Team of Teams: New Rules of Engagement for a Complex World*, Portfolio Penguin, London.

8 Extra-Dependent Team development

Developing teams within the system

Extra-Dependent Teams only exist because they work with Inter-Dependent Teams. Developing an Extra-Dependent Team therefore cannot be done in isolation because it inevitably affects the people outside the team. In this respect most team-development models are limited because their focus is *inside* the team. Considering the development of Extra-Dependent Teams therefore needs an approach based on systems thinking.

One of the most influential thinkers on team development within systems is Peter Hawkins. His work (Hawkins and Smith, 2006; Hawkins, 2011; Hawkins (ed), 2014) has encouraged many practitioners, including myself, to think outside of the team and see it within the wider system – including its connections with other teams, the rest of the organisation, other organisations and beyond into society. He says he 'gradually came to realize that the performance of a team is not transformed just by the team relating well internally, for the team performance is fundamentally dependent on how the team collectively engages with all its stakeholders' (Hawkins, 2011, p. 34).

Hawkins doesn't distinguish between Inter-Dependent or Extra-Dependent Teams, but the nature of his systemic approach provides clear opportunities for appreciating the connections between the two types of team and encourages learning and action to generate changes and development. For Extra-Dependent Teams, this systemic perspective is vital. Without it, development of the team becomes an inward-looking, self-interested pursuit that is often tangential to the purpose of the organisation. Yet with it, Extra-Dependent Teams become collaborative, constructive and embedded with Inter-Dependent Teams. They are also more able to identify, negotiate and realise their combined capability in partnership with Inter-Dependent Teams so that they contribute strategic value to the heart of an organisation's activity and ultimately to the organisation's customers. But to do this, Extra-Dependent Teams need to develop fundamentally differently from Inter-Dependent Teams. And because learning is a core dynamic in Extra-Dependent Teams, developing them is akin to learning to learn. There is therefore a lot to cover in this chapter.

Firstly I introduce a plural mental model of team development that distinguishes between developing an Inter-Dependent Team compared to developing an Extra-Dependent Team. Core to developing an Extra-Dependent Team is learning better together. This calls for collaborative learning and I use the example of a dysfunctional Extra-Dependent Team of matrons within a hospital to explain what can practically be done. Yet behind the practicalities is a need to understand the deeper learning processes going on between people – the exchange of both explicit and tacit knowledge. I cover this before listing some practical activities that can be done to support such collaborative learning. Finally in this chapter, I explain that the development of the team is directly related to the quality of learning going on within the Extra-Dependent Team and use a number of practical examples to highlight three levels of learning. At the simplest level learning is about *implementing* what is required. But to develop the team needs to *improve* what it does. However, the greatest quality of learning is *innovative* learning, where core assumptions are challenged and changed so that better things can be done. This level of learning is crucial to appreciate as it not only affects the Extra-Dependent Team, it also impacts the wider organisation, and even other people beyond the organisation. It therefore provides a type of team synergy that can impact an entire marketplace.

Developing Extra-Dependent Teams

The team performance curve of Katzenbach and Smith (1993) gives a clear sense of the link between working together better as a team and an increase in team performance. But since Extra-Dependent Teams improve through learning better together, they need a very different performance curve.

Figure 8.1 shows the plural team development curve. On the right-hand-side, performance is improved through developing the team as an Inter-Dependent Team by working better together to achieve a common goal. It is very similar to the team performance curve (Katzenbach & Smith, 1993). But the plural team development curve also branches off to the left – where the team performance curve only stops at working group. On this left-hand side, performance is improved through developing the team as an Extra-Dependent Team by learning better together to develop a common practice.

The central point on the horizontal axis of Figure 8.1 is where clarity is required around what type of team it is and therefore how it can be developed. Without this clarity, the team runs the risk of deviating from its natural team dynamic and becoming confused. This stage is therefore called the dysfunctional team stage. It is similar to the pseudo team of Katzenbach and Smith's team performance curve, where teams try to *act* like an Inter-Dependent Team, but don't *perform* like one. In the plural team development model, this dysfunctional team stage is most likely the result of an Extra-Dependent Team trying to act like an Inter-Dependent Team but that

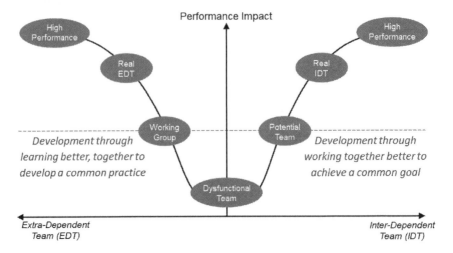

Figure 8.1 The plural team development curve.

through doing so, it impacts performance. This is often expressed as 'the problem is the team isn't a team'.

This dysfunctional team stage is where Steve's team in Chapter 1 ended up *because* of the team development that it went through. At the start of the development the consultant team diagnosed themselves as a working group. As the team developed to try to work together better through differences and common goals, so the team started to become increasingly dysfunctional. But rather than coming out the other side of the dip and reaching the potential team stage as expected by the Team School, the team got stuck in the dysfunctional team stage because its natural dynamics of similarity started to compete with the imposed structures of difference.

Steve didn't have the plural team development curve when he decided to develop the consultant team. If he had, he might have recognised that the working group was already a step towards being a real Extra-Dependent Team. For working groups, the prospect of synergy isn't actually very far away. But to move along this development line requires the Extra-Dependent Team to learn better together rather than work together better.

Learning better together: a dysfunctional Extra-Dependent Team of matrons

Over many years I have had the pleasure to develop professionals within a particular hospital within the National Health Service (NHS). The more that I worked with these professionals, the more I realised that many of them were line managed as an Extra-Dependent Team. This contrasted with the way they were being encouraged to perform in order to support person-centred coordinated care. That is, they needed to perform in multi-disciplinary teams that spanned different departments and even different agencies (NHS England, 2014). Multidisciplinary teams are a great example of Inter-Dependent Teams. But whilst the NHS attempts to perform through Inter-Dependent Teams, its line management is invariably structured around Extra-Dependent Teams.

An opportunity emerged to develop a team of matrons in the hospital. Technically, the 20 matrons were split into five different healthcare groups, each with a different line manager. But following a Care Quality Commission (CQC) inspection a clear need had been identified that the matrons within the hospital were collectively underperforming and the hospital decided to develop them – as a team. The perceived priority was to decide on a common set of standards as it gave a clear reference point against which to assess their development progress. At first this appeared easy as standards had already been drafted. But after six months no progress had been made because they couldn't agree on them. The managers of the matrons got increasingly frustrated, seeing the lack of progress as indicative of the matrons' problems – they just couldn't work together as a team. The conventional mental model of teams was very much in the driving seat and both the managers and the matrons themselves saw the team as dysfunctional but with no clear way forward.

With the plural mental model it was easier to see what the problem was. The matrons were an Extra-Dependent Team and not an Inter-Dependent Team. As such, they worked apart, not together, and this was entirely functional and to be expected. But consequently the matrons had *never* had the chance to all get together to discuss or agree on any standards and this was *not* functional as an Extra-Dependent Team. Of course, the matrons' managers could have created the conditions for them to meet, but instead expected them to do it themselves, and when the matrons didn't it was further evidence to the managers that the matrons' team was dysfunctional. But with the Hawkins' systemic perspective, it indicated that not only were the matrons dysfunctional, so too was their relationship with their respective line managers. In effect, the line managers were perpetuating the dysfunction within the matrons by expecting impossible things of them. A development approach was therefore needed that allowed learning to be collaborative whilst encouraging collective change of the shared repertoire.

Collaborative learning

For the past two decades I have used action learning to support the collaborative development of people who don't work together but who do similar work, typically managers learning together to manage better. I had also demonstrated action learning within a workshop on Extra-Dependent Teams at the same hospital about a year before. One of the participants had described it as 'magic in the room' because it was so powerful. For me, it is the simplest way for supporting collaborative learning in an Extra-Dependent Team.

Action learning, as briefly introduced in Chapter 2, involves learning together in groups on real problems that require action and for which there
is no clear answer. It works because the learning group collectively has
combined knowledge, varied experiences and multiple perspectives about
a repertoire of work that they share. This enables an individual's problem
to be explored amongst the group for everyone's mutual benefit. One person
shares a challenge and the group explores it together, with everyone learning
from the questions, challenges and reflections shared by the group. During
several iterations of this process with different people sharing different real
challenges, everyone learns together. As a learning process, it is both powerful and simple and as a result is seen as one of the most significant forms
of personal and organisational development to emerge over the last few decades (Pedler, 2008). It has also been described as 'perhaps the most widely
known form of learning group coaching in the UK' (Thornton, 2016, p. 152).
It remains a potent collaborative learning approach and one suited for supporting the sharing of repertoire in an Extra-Dependent Team.

But for collaborative learning to work within this team, everyone needed
to be a willing and responsible participant. Unfortunately, I had identified
that there was an embedded sense of victimhood in the matrons' shared
repertoire that would limit the potential of the learning.

Victimhood within the shared repertoire

I had first noticed a communal sense of victimhood when discussing with
the matrons how they wanted the programme to work. Prior to this they
had all felt like the development of the team was being done *to* them – not
by them. They showed strong signs of identifying together as victims –
lacking influence, having to follow orders, constantly fire-fighting. It was
clearly one of the things that they *had* managed to learn socially together as
an Extra-Dependent Team. The problem with identifying as victims in an
Extra-Dependent Team is that learning, identity, meaning and practice are
all interwoven into the shared repertoire. In effect, the matrons were sharing their victimhood with each other informally, *learning* from each other's experience as victims, *identifying* with each other's helpless situation,
drawing *meaning* from this that they were dysfunctional as a matron team
and embedded that into their *practice* by doing what they were told and just
getting on with the job as best they could. Their shared repertoire was as
much about being a victim as it was about being a matron. They had begun
to identify one with the other through their social learning together and
it was negatively affecting their combined capability, as the CQC proved
and the subsequent report damaged their team reputation. The way to address their performance was for them to learn better together to develop
their common practice. Through sharing their repertoire and building their
combined capability they would start to enhance their reputation. It meant
meeting formally.

As the handful of matrons and I met for the first meeting I was keen to ensure they remained in the driving seat. I asked them what they wanted to achieve through the meetings we had planned, what they wanted the standards for and how they expected them to be used. As we discussed these topics in turn, it was clear that the standards could only progress, for them, when all the matrons discussed them together at the same time in the same place. Prompting them to take action, a date was agreed and invitations were sent to all the matrons to attend a whole-day event the following month.

Designing the development

I designed the day with Extra-Dependent Teams in the forefront of my mind. This meant learning better together, not getting stuck in arguing decisions. So I decided to help proceedings in three ways:

1   Firstly, I would dedicate most of the morning to allowing the matrons to learn from each other. This would be at a fairly basic level as they needed to feel at ease with each other first. I also wanted to help them identify their similarities rather than what they had continuously focused on so far – pointing out their differences.
2   Secondly, the standards would need to be agreed with their managers after the meeting, and having identified that the matrons' relationship with them was part of the dysfunction, I decided to build this agreement process into the agenda. It would mean inviting the managers into the room towards the end of the day for the matrons to present their proposed standards. Not only would it provide a 'hard stop' to the day reducing the chances of procrastination, it would also provide an opportunity for both sides to clarify any misunderstandings that the matrons might have of what their managers expected of them.
3   Finally, I was clear with myself and the matrons that the standards document would form only a fraction of the total matrons' shared repertoire. Yet the learning process would share repertoire more rich than the standards document. For instance, *the way* that the standards were agreed on the day was as important to developing the shared repertoire as what was *written in* the standards. Indeed, the *story* of how the day went and the standards themselves would each be concrete representations of their common practice and evidence of their learning better together. They would represent a specific story about a moment in time when the matrons and their managers agreed. It would acknowledge similarity amongst the matrons and it would demonstrate progress as a team. Sharing the repertoire in this way would lead to a small shift in the team's reputation – their identity. They would move from victims in the chaos of the hospital to shapers of the hospital's improved future.

The scene was set.

Learning from similarity

Nearly all the matrons attended the meeting. After a short introduction re-minding them about Extra-Dependent Teams and urging them to focus on their similarities rather than differences, they all got down to the activity of sharing experiences with each other. This was done in groups of three people, deliberately splitting up the people who knew each other well. Each group of three had selected one of five priorities that the hospital had identified as a result of the last CQC inspection. The matrons wanted their standards to be defined around these priorities. Everyone was simply asked to share an experience in their groups of what they did that they felt addressed that pri-ority in their work. The other two were invited to ask questions or share their thoughts on how it could be standardised with their own experiences. It all led to a rich sharing of repertoire which culminated in a plenary session sharing the key output from each three-person group that formed a rough draft of the standards.

A review at the end of the morning showed great progress, but still some victimhood:

- 'I'm amazed at how similar we are.'
- 'I hadn't realised quite how much we do that is the same.'
- 'Ditto, I agree with everything others have said.'
- 'I'm nervous we don't have time to pull the standards together before the [senior managers] arrive later.'

Shifts in the team's dynamics

The first half of the afternoon was focused on agreeing the specific text of the standards. Having got them to acknowledge similarity, the discussion was collaborative and focused. The team started to identify themselves as influential players and encourage each other, even challenging victim be-liefs when they occasionally emerged. During one such exchange, an elder in the team verbalised their belief that nothing would change because of 'them' – the managers. But this was challenged by a newcomer who said that the relationship she had with her senior manager was both construc-tive and similar to relationships she'd had in the previous hospital she worked in. This prompted other matrons to support the newcomer's posi-tion. It was an important shift in dynamics – the newcomer was inbound whilst the elder was outbound. As a result, it was an important shift in the team's identity.

In the final half hour before the senior managers arrived, the matrons pulled together a presentation and arranged themselves ready to share. It was clear from how they arranged themselves to present as a team that they realised their reputation was in the spotlight.

Ownership of the common practice

I had been clear all along with everyone that this was the matrons' event, inspired and organised by them. The matrons therefore owned the meeting space and were to host their managers, rather than the other way around. The managers would only come into the room once the matrons were ready. This was important because if the matrons owned the space, the meeting and the process, they would also own the common practice. This was made all the more important because the managers all had nursing backgrounds – indeed, some had been matrons in the past. So not only did they have power through their senior positions, they had knowledge and experience of the work that the matrons did. This power was likely a key part of what lay behind the victimhood that the matrons identified with. So to shift the identity away from victimhood and into influence, the matrons would need to own the common practice. They had to present the standards as if they were their own – because they were.

Shifting the shared repertoire

The final hour and a half were compelling to witness. The matrons asserted themselves. The newcomer matron who had challenged the elder volunteered to represent the team and share the standards with the managers, but all matrons were present and contributed by supporting the representative. With a newcomer representing them, the language, posture, approach and tone were all different from the victimhood of before. They were composed, considered, responsible, authoritative, collaborative and strategic. Indeed, they were demonstrating many of the behaviours that were represented in their standards.

The managers reciprocated. The subsequent discussion was adult, respectful and progressive. The managers accepted the standards in principle pending some minor changes, ironically even inviting them to add more assertive language. The team had clearly achieved something that they had failed to achieve in the previous eight months. They were acting as a whole team, speaking up for each other, collaborating, listening, building, progressing. As they shifted their shared repertoire in front of their own and their managers' eyes, they were shifting the relationship between each other. Everyone in the room, both inside and outside the team, could see that the matrons could be different. The team had started to develop.

Developing through learning better together

Using the plural team development curve the matron team had shown strong signs of progressing from a dysfunctional team to a working group. Note that at no point was there any discussion about a common goal and there was no expectation from me for them to try to work together between meetings. Rather, the team needed structured time in order to learn together. Extra-Dependent Teams learn through the collaborative conversion of explicit and tacit knowledge. *Explicit* knowledge is transmittable in formal, systematic language and is typically the type of knowledge we are taught in schools and universities. This compares to *tacit* knowledge which is personal, context-specific and therefore hard to formalise or communicate. A physiotherapist's knowledge, for instance, is not just within her head, it is also within her hands. She feels the fibres of a patient's body in order to experience where the work needs to be done before shaping her hand automatically and applying the right pressure in the right direction to follow the muscle. She's thinking of course and could tell the patient what she's doing, but a great deal of the knowledge comes from the experience of feeling lots of different bodies over many years. So what she shares explicitly is only the tip of the knowledge iceberg because so much of her practice is tacit. The shared repertoire within an Extra-Dependent Team is made up of similar explicit and tacit knowledge. Some of it is communicable, but a great deal of it is not. For instance, writing matron standards is explicit knowledge but what it takes to present these standards confidently and assertively in front of peers takes tacit knowledge.

Tacit and explicit knowledge are mutually complementary entities (Nonaka and Takeuchi, 1995). They both interact and interchange with each other as a social exchange process *between* individuals. It is a collaborative process of *knowledge conversion* that stimulates learning within the team. Nonaka and Takeuchi (1995) identify four modes of knowledge conversion, shown in Table 8.1.

Combination

Combination is the most widely recognised mode of knowledge conversion. It involves the conversion of explicit knowledge to explicit knowledge. An example of this mode is here in this paragraph. I have received explicit knowledge from the work of Nonaka and Takeuchi and am converting it into explicit knowledge around how to understand Extra-Dependent Teams. Explicit knowledge includes emails, meetings, telephone conversations and data on computer systems as well as many other forms. In the matron

Table 8.1 Nonaka and Takeuchi's four modes of knowledge conversion

From	To	Mode
Explicit knowledge	*Explicit knowledge*	Combination
Explicit knowledge	*Tacit knowledge*	Internalisation
Tacit knowledge	*Tacit knowledge*	Socialisation
Tacit knowledge	*Explicit knowledge*	Externalisation

example, the hospital's priorities were converted into the matrons' standards. The explicit sharing of repertoire had converted into explicit standards through the process of combination.

Internalisation

This is the conversion of knowledge from explicit to tacit. It is closely related to learning by doing. For instance, simple guidance from elders is converted into action by newcomers through applying the guidance in their practice. This internalises the knowledge. Explicit verbal or written knowledge therefore converts into contextualised, difficult-to-describe learning. In a meeting where an Extra-Dependent Team is learning together it might be witnessed as take-away actions at the end of a meeting[1] or it might be evident in a subsequent meeting when a review of actions since last time highlights experiences of those actions. Ultimately, it's not the act of discussing that is internalising, but the act of *doing* what has been discussed.

Socialisation

Socialisation is a conversion of tacit knowledge to tacit knowledge. Nothing is explicit. It's typically a process of copying through observation, imitation and application to practice. It's the sort of knowledge that represents the 'culture' of a team. As such it's difficult to pinpoint, yet easy to grasp. The matron team development outlined above highlights the importance of this mode. The knowledge of victimhood was embedded tacitly through socialisation outside of team meetings. It might have happened as matrons passed each other in corridors and shared the latest cost cut, or senior manager directive, and responded with a rolling of eyes, a shake of the head or a frustrated throwaway comment. For the same reasons it was important for all the matrons to observe the newcomer being confident, assertive and influential so that they too might learn tacitly to do the same. Socialisation is learning carried through the emotion of experience but cuts to the heart of the meaning of the common practice.

Externalisation

The conversion of knowledge from tacit to explicit is called externalisation. This is the type of knowledge shared when one person is responding to other people's inquisitive questioning. It is a process that helps clarify unformed thoughts, implicit beliefs and emergent ideas. It occurs when people feel safe with the questioners and the questioners have the other person's interests at heart. The questioners appreciate that the person in the spotlight hasn't yet clarified the tacit knowledge within them and the line of questioning is the process required to help surface this tacit knowledge and turn it into explicit knowledge – which forms the answer to the question.

Questions need to be shaped in order to probe the tacit knowledge within the other person and the listening needs to enable them to articulate this authentically – so the *meaning* is shared, not just the words. The sort of questions that gently probe might include:

- How would you describe what's going on in that project?
- Where are things working well?
- When do you struggle most?
- How do you make sense of the situation?
- What do you think the causes might be?
- What are you hoping to achieve?
- How does this reflect who you are?

Externalisation is a form of awareness raising which is a key process in both coaching (Downey, 2003) and action learning (Revans, 1982). Through externalisation people learn for themselves about themselves. In the team context, such learning helps form meaning of common problems and situations. It builds a sense of connection, cohesion and identity. It helps develop the common practice.

Sufficient amounts of safety need to be created in the team for such learning to occur (Thornton, 2016). The team needs to trust each other to open up and be honest about their situation, their thoughts and themselves. The safety needs to be assured right across the team so that everyone feels valued and able to share what they know, what they're thinking, how they are feeling, what they hope for and what concerns them. Yet the team meeting is not an accountability-free zone. Individuals will be taking actions for which they are individually responsible and which constitute their performance. A team manager needs to create conditions in the team that means it is *safe enough* for learning together, but not so safe that action isn't possible. It's a difficult balance to strike, but if people aren't sharing then it is a clear indicator that safety is insufficient. In my experience of collaborative learning and team coaching, safety typically takes time to build up with team members sharing relatively trivial knowledge in the first few meetings before really opening up to the riskier, deeper, more valuable learning later on. Managers facilitating such meetings need to be patient.

Learning to meet together: meeting to learn together

The matrons team had learned the value of meeting together. But they are not alone in needing to learn to meet. Many of the various Extra-Dependent Teams that I have witnessed over the years have had challenges with meeting. To become functional, the team needs to learn to meet and it's vital that the reason to meet is to learn. As Erik found in his engineer team meetings, there is insufficient value in trying to use meetings to coordinate activities and as Steve found in his team of training consultants and the matrons found when trying to get together, the work going on outside the team is sometimes too demanding to spare the time to meet. But what helps is ensuring that the meeting is to learn together because then everyone feels personal and collective value gained from the meeting. Learning is how Extra-Dependent Teams develop their practice and add the value they need to, and thus benefit the places where they perform. Extra-Dependent Team members need to experience real value through learning together so that they *choose* to meet together rather than prioritise other work and avoid meeting. When learning is directly relevant to their work and team members improve their combined capability as a result, they can appreciate how meeting will benefit their performance. They can then excuse themselves from their work with people outside the team, knowing full well that their absence will likely benefit these same people in due course.

Facilitating the learning of the team is a key skill for a team manager to learn and uses the skills outlined in Chapter 6. A simple approach that I have experimented with over the last few years is doing 'rounds' of the team, whereby each person takes it in turn to share something. A meeting would then consist of a series of rounds: a round for introductions, a round of reflection, a round of actions and so on. Rounds help bring variety, balance and fairness to the meeting process and ensure that no one dominates discussions, or that anyone is left out. It helps build safety through a gradual and balanced process of sharing amongst everyone. Elders, newcomers, Core, Active or Peripheral members can all contribute to the learning of the team and should all be involved.

Below are some suggested approaches that can be used in rounds, but this is by no means an exhaustive list.

Learning objectives

In a collaborative learning environment everyone can be expected to have their own learning objective – there is no need for everyone to have the same learning objective. When that happens it's a good indication that the learning is didactic (teaching or instructing) and, by definition, not collaborative. Asking team members what they want to learn helps bring collective focus to what needs to happen to ensure the learning is rewarding. Sharing learning objectives can be a process of combination or indeed of externalisation depending on the level of consideration prior to the meeting. Either way it is useful for learning objectives to be limited to one or two short sentences so that they are easily referred to during the meeting as the learning happens.

Sharing successes

This allows everyone to share something that they are proud of in the work that they are currently doing. This is not an 'update for your information', but a constructive share for collective learning through combination. It might be that it is nothing new, but it helps reinforce the existing shared repertoire and confirms its value. Because success is typically positive, people find it easier to disclose than topics that are negative about themselves. So it's a really helpful round to have early in a team meeting because it can be a relatively quick process and provides an opportunity for everyone to get actively involved in the learning from the start.

At a deeper level, it helps reinforce a sense of identity and practice as the team's shared repertoire is exchanged openly with evidence of performance impact. Because members rarely work together, such evidence is not easily witnessed, so sharing openly builds a broader understanding of the repertoire and its benefits.

It's useful to keep the process quite light with only a few short exchanges such as questions and answers, so that everyone is involved and no one dominates too soon. This sets the scene for balanced contributions for the rest of the meeting.

Work reviews

There is much to be learned from reviewing the work that an Extra-Dependent Team member does with other people outside the team. It shines a light on the combined capability at work and represents an *example* of what everyone is involved in. It therefore provides an opportunity to share knowledge together across the full breadth or depth of the shared repertoire. Reviews can be done at any point. They do not have to wait until the work is complete.

It works by a team member taking the spotlight (this could be a 'round' that covers multiple meetings rather than cramming everyone's turn into one meeting). They prepare beforehand and then deliver at the meeting a short summary (c. five minutes) of what their work has involved. A concise summary is important to avoid a monologue and ensure there is time to exchange learning between team members. Exchange can be prompted in two ways: the other team members ask questions of the person in order to explore the areas of the work that are of most interest to them; and/or the person themselves can ask questions of the rest of the team to help appreciate their repertoire. Questions the person might ask of the team might include:

- What else might I have done at this point?
- What would others have done differently?
- I've done [this] and I'm therefore expecting [that]. From your experience what else might I expect to happen?
- I found [this part] particularly difficult. What do others do that makes [this part] easier?

Similarly, questions from the team can help to make the learning more relevant to them. Example questions include:

- How did you find it most useful to approach the work?
- How did you find the new technology helped?
- What did you find most difficult?
- Some of us have never done this sort of work before. How would you suggest we approach it for the first time?

The review becomes a live case study around which to share learning, explore possibilities, prompt action and build shared repertoire.

Exploring an individual's challenge

This technique is most like the challenges used within action learning. It involves team members sharing with the team a situation that they currently have which they are finding challenging and for which there is no clear way forward. Because of the common practice, it is often the case that such challenges are experienced by others within the team, or indeed have yet to experience such a challenge. Exploring such challenges benefits everyone in developing the team's combined capability.

Open discussion helps bring the whole team's wisdom and experience to bear on the specific challenge. A similar questioning approach to those of the work reviews is used to stimulate discussion and interaction. It might also involve a round of reflection (see below) in order to capture multiple thoughts and ideas. But at the end, the action to be taken to move the challenge forward is the individual's because in an Extra-Dependent Team it's the individual who is accountable for the work that they do. However, in the interests of the Extra-Dependent Team learning together to develop a common practice, the results of such actions should be brought back to the team meeting at a later date for everyone to appreciate its impact and effectiveness. This then allows individual actions to remain the individual's responsibility, but for the whole team to benefit from the learning that results from it – whether it is successful or not. The common practice therefore remains in the hands of the team, whilst the performance remains in the hands of the individual.

Exploring common challenges

This is similar to exploring an individual's challenge, but the challenge has already been recognised as something everyone in the team experiences. An example of this might be the introduction of new technology, or a change in the organisational structure which results in a need to change elements of the shared repertoire. It's an opportunity for the manager to lead a discussion on how the team as a whole should agree to do its work. In effect it involves renegotiating the agreed norms of the shared repertoire so that everyone overcomes the challenge in the same way. It enables elders as well as newcomers to propose optional ways forward based on a mix of experience on the same issue. Perhaps this challenge has happened in the past and the elder can share the history of what the team learned to do the last time it happened. Or a newcomer might have experienced something similar in a previous role or organisation which helps appreciate some of the factors that this new challenge presents.

Different members of the team might opt to actively experiment with different options in a coordinated manner. This allows the team to be inventive in its approach, not having to make decisions without first trying them out. Experimentation also restricts individual divergence from the shared repertoire to the temporary period of the experiment.

Because Extra-Dependent Teams work with others outside the team, exploring common challenges should also include how team members get along with the Inter-Dependent Teams that they play a part in. For instance, whilst Erik's engineering team liked to focus its attention on the subject of engineering, some of the team's greatest challenges were around getting along with other disciplines in the Inter-Dependent Teams. At one meeting I prompted the engineers to discuss a common challenge and they identified a major issue: attendance at project manager meetings. The engineers all experienced some degree of frustration around the way that project managers ran their meetings. Core to the issue was whether the engineer should have to stay for the whole meeting or whether they could be there 'for just their part'. This was a common challenge that formed part of the shared repertoire of the engineering team and the discussion was crucial for the team's performance and reputation. Interestingly, as some people vented their frustrations around project managers, others shared how they either negotiated their attendance with project managers, or ensured they drew value from their full attendance at a meeting. The reflections at the end indicated that it had generated some ideas for dealing with the issue, but that the value of attendance was reinforced. This was important so that the Extra-Dependent Team didn't lose sight of the fact that they could only perform when they worked productively with others outside the team.

Active experimentation

Professional bodies, original ideas, new research and innovative technologies are constantly prompting us to rethink how we do things. This is matched by the constant changes occurring within organisations. Extra-Dependent Teams become aware of such changes through:

- the manager updating the team on bigger picture issues;
- team members informed of changes in the course of their work with others outside the team;

- team members discovering new thinking from attending courses, conferences or in the course of their professional reading;
- newcomers explaining novel approaches they have used in different organisations.

Adopting new ideas without experimenting with them first risks authoritarian decision making which erodes the collective ownership of the common practice. Experimenting involves a deliberate and coordinated approach to one or more team members piloting a new method during a temporary period. Those involved in the pilot (typically people outside the team) can be informed of the temporary change and can be involved in assessing the pilot's success. The pilot then provides an opportunity for the team to learn collectively before agreeing a permanent change to the shared repertoire.

Experimentation may be rapid – a short change in action that is trialled by one team member with the results shared quickly with the rest of the team – or might involve a more prolonged process. Regular sharing of progress of the experiment ensures that the team continues to value the different approach of the experimenter as well as ensuring the experimenter remains part of the team as 'one of us' rather than becoming peripheral and perhaps even 'one of them'.

Reflection

A simple, but underused technique to facilitate learning during meetings is reflection. Reflection is the externalisation process of knowledge conversion highlighted above. It allows tacit, inexplicable knowledge to be accessed, processed and then articulated as explicit knowledge to the individual reflecting, or other people in the team when this reflection is shared. Reflection can be rapid and simple, perhaps bringing focus on specific actions that everyone needs to clarify before leaving a meeting. But it can also be deep and meaningful, addressing foundational aspects of the common practice and enabling fundamental shifts in identity and meaning. Reflection can be done by individuals in silence or in pairs or small groups. To ensure that reflection becomes tangible it is useful to have everyone share their own thoughts in a round. If this is at the end of a meeting and there is limited time, then it can help to share a key action, or a few words, or even to get everyone to write their reflection down. I've learned over the years that this last technique captures much, much more for the individual than asking only to share verbally.

With the exploration and experimentation amongst the team, the shared repertoire is stretched and expanded to suit the demands of a developing organisational context. Learning together evens out differences within the team, sharing one person's strength to help improve another person's weakness. Through this process greater consistency amongst the team is achieved and with it the combined capability of the team is increased. As outlined in

Chapter 4, this combined capability is deployed through each individual. When a team member leaves a meeting, he or she will have grown in combined capability because of the collaborative learning that occurred. This is how the synergy of the team is generated. They then take that improved combined capability into their performance when working with others outside the team.

Developing synergy in Extra-Dependent Teams

A tool that I have found useful to support the development of Extra-Dependent Teams is Boydell and Leary's performance model (Boydell and Leary, 1996). I have adapted it here, but it retains the original three levels of improvement. The levels can be directly mapped onto the plural team development curve as in Table 8.2.

When an Extra-Dependent Team starts to share their repertoire together in the ways that I have outlined above, they learn better together and start to improve their combined capability. They develop and implement new ways of operating and introduce new equipment, tools or methods for providing their combined capability. When this improved combined capability is delivered outside the team, it has a consequent impact on the organisation. But when an Extra-Dependent Team is high performing, they are learning at a depth that addresses shared assumptions about their common practice and start to develop and experiment with new shared repertoire that has the capability of shifting the marketplace within which the organisation sits. Below is an explanation of each type of learning with examples of how it is done and the effect it has.

Learning better together: example of improving

The following case is an example of improving because the impact of learning was felt outside the team. We return to Malinda's risk-management team. As head of risk, Malinda was charged with developing a strategy to change the way that risk was managed across the organisation (see more on this in Chapter 9). Too much basic risk management was being left to the specialist risk analysts and regional risk managers to do, leaving more complex risks being unmanaged in each region. It was an unsustainable situation which

Table 8.2 Levels of synergy

Level	Combined capability	What it achieves	Impact	Synergy
Working group	Implementing	Doing things well	Team	$1+1+1=3$
Real EDT	Improving	Doing things better	Organisation	$1+1+1=6$
High-performing EDT	Innovating	Doing better things	Market	$1+1+1=$ WOW!

needed to be addressed in a strategic way. A strategy had been developed by Malinda and cascaded, but it had got stuck at the first hurdle – the regional risk managers themselves – due to the different requirements of the different regions. So she altered the strategy and tasked each regional risk manager to develop their own individual plans and agree them directly with the respective regional director.

This was an opportunity for shared learning within the team. Whatever each region thought about their own exceptional circumstances, there were going to be plenty of similarities in many of the issues, arguments, approaches and methods. A 'learning share' meeting was organised. Initially, regional risk managers were uncertain about the value because, they 'hadn't written it yet, so I have nothing to share'. But the learning share meeting would only work if they *hadn't* completed it. For the learning to be valuable, their options had to remain open and therefore not yet complete.

The meeting was voluntary and most of them attended. The 'rounds' approach was used to shape the meeting. After some scene setting and agreeing how they would work together (open, honest, collaborative, etc.), everyone clarified their 'personal objectives' for the event. This was followed by a second round which created a priority of topics that everyone wished to learn about and address. Four of the nine who attended volunteered to speak on behalf of these topics using the technique of exploring an individual's challenge. The time allowed approximately 40 minutes per person.

For each topic discussion, the same process was followed, but with a different person in the spotlight. There was a tremendous exchange of explicit and tacit knowledge for all who attended. It was the first time that the group had taken part in learning like this and so it was a little clunky at times. Indeed, one person coincidentally described the process as a bit like 'herding cats'! It made me smile.

Even so, some good listening and questioning from everyone provided sufficient progress during the day for people to see clear value. Comments from team members at the end of the learning share event included:

- 'A clear way forwards, as a team!! Full participation from all attendees. Clear actions taken and agreement for completion. People taking ownership and accountability.'
- 'Awareness that what we are delivering [in our region] is going in the right direction. A clear improvement action plan to act upon.'
- 'I can learn from others, but do my own thing.'
- 'Recognised that the [regional risk managers] work to deliver their own customers' agenda but use common processes.'

Soon after this learning share event took place, the regional plans were finalised and agreed with the respective regions. Whilst each was slightly different, it provided a clear agreement for each regional risk manager with their respective Inter-Dependent Team on how they would work together.

The team were improving through learning better together and their impact would now be felt much more across the organisation.

This example shows that learning together provided the conditions for every member of the Extra-Dependent Team to increase their combined capability and then apply that combined capability uniquely to their area of responsibility. Each member of the Extra-Dependent Team was more capable and more confident to do their own thing locally because of what they had learned together. They had demonstrated that they could improve through learning together. They were becoming a real Extra-Dependent Team.

Learning even better together: example of innovating

The innovating level of learning within Extra-Dependent Teams has the potential to deliver significant performance due to their connections across the wider system. Because Extra-Dependent Teams engage with multiple Inter-Dependent Teams across organisations, should they innovate their common practice, it would have an effect on all these Inter-Dependent Teams. For instance, should Malinda's team have developed a new, simpler method of assessing budgetary risk, her team would have deployed that within all the regional teams across the UK. If this new method stimulated an improvement in the accuracy or effectiveness of the regional teams to manage or mitigate risk, then the whole organisation would have improved in some small but significant part. And because the specialist construction organisation had customers and stakeholders within the broader system, the effect of this new method would have provided the organisation with an edge within the marketplace. In effect, innovative learning within the Extra-Dependent Team can have a system-wide impact.

What makes learning innovating rather than just improving is the degree to which the team challenges and overcomes the assumed ways of doing things. This level of learning is referred to as double-loop learning (Argyris, 1994) where underlying assumptions, policies and norms are questioned and addressed in a process of learning that is more profound – doing better things. Such learning allows for inventive new practices which can be introduced by all Extra-Dependent Team members to all Inter-Dependent Teams across an organisation and beyond. But this learning is rare, not only because it is challenging to do, but also because defensive behaviours within the culture of the team prevent the openness and rigour to question. Such behaviours include self-protection, maximising winning, minimising losing and minimising negative emotions. It means that underperformance and mistakes are not explored as a legitimate source of team learning. Yet when they are they can be sources of deep learning for everyone.

For instance, I had been coaching a dysfunctional Extra-Dependent Team for some time, making very good progress through working group towards a real Extra-Dependent Team. However, as with the reality of complex organisations, an incident occurred which caused the manager to have to move roles. The incident was symptomatic of the challenges, and also the potential, that the innovation level of learning offers and I share the story to highlight what this involves.

The team managed anti-money-laundering (AML) operations within a financial services organisation. It was a characteristic Extra-Dependent Team made up of AML officers who all did similar work but each operated in a different country, so team members rarely worked with each other. Instead, they worked with people outside the team such as the respective organisation's country head, the local police and the local regulator. All these stakeholders had a vested interest in reducing money-laundering activity within their respective country, but for different reasons. So whilst they weren't in any way an Inter-Dependent Team as convention defines it, they were each playing a different role in trying to reach the same goal – the reduction of money-laundering activity. With such access to people outside the organisation, the quality of team members' relationships with external stakeholders was a strategic part of the shared repertoire of the team.

George was a relatively new member of the team, but as manager, his experience and individual repertoire had meant he was inbound and in his first six months with the team had become a Core member. He was therefore pushing the boundaries of the shared repertoire of the existing team with techniques, methods and knowledge that the existing team members didn't have.

One such area of the shared repertoire that George was trying to develop was the way an AML officer responded to requests by the local police to submit evidence about the financial transactions of people the police suspected of money-laundering activity. If the police were investigating a suspect, then they wanted to know about their financial history and approached financial organisations to get them to submit evidence. The police in George's country of responsibility were using a method for requesting evidence that was very casual and therefore open to misuse. In particular, George was concerned that it risked breaching the organisation's legal responsibilities to the customer regarding data protection. George's previous experience in other countries was for the police to follow more stringent procedures which would allow him to comply with their needs, but without compromising customers' data privacy. So when George refused his country's police request for financial data about a suspect without sufficient safeguards to protect the suspect, it led to some significant disagreements with the local authorities.

Whilst George attempted to work with the police to improve their standards to meet his own (and the norm in many other countries), the country regulator sided with the police and left George in a difficult position. George's country manager saw an opportunity to reach agreement with all stakeholders and asked George to comply. George was left with a moral dilemma: to lower his standards for treating suspects and keep his job, or maintain his standards and lose his job. It was a big call and George decided to keep his standards. It meant he had to leave his job as manager of the team.

Such was the sensitivity of this issue that George's immediate reaction was to keep things quiet. However, I challenged him on this assumption, explaining that the relationship with external stakeholders was a key part of the shared repertoire of the team and that each and every other AML officer experienced similar relationship issues with their own country manager, police and regulator. Whilst it appeared that George's country was the only one with the lower standards, all AML officers could learn from the experience.

A lessons-learned session was run with the focus on everyone learning together, rather than trying to identify what George himself should have done differently. The session put George in a challenging position because it disclosed to the rest of the team his full repertoire involved in the incident. Yet this candidness overcame the limiting factors of defensive routines and allowed the team to appreciate the skills, approaches, conversations, stories and the resolve George had used to influence the situation – sometimes successfully, but ultimately unsuccessfully. From this disclosure, the team could learn collaboratively about how to change things.

This is where this example has the potential for innovative learning. Whilst the situation couldn't be changed, the rest of the team could learn together about how to better influence external stakeholder relationships such that standards could be maintained. The main assumption to overcome was the team's belief that they couldn't change an external stakeholder's way of working. George's determined approach had started to challenge this and made some initial movement with the police in raising their standards. But insufficient attention had been given to the regulator and internal stakeholders who might have supported this effort and this was an area for the team to learn from.

If the outcome had been different, George would have significantly altered the way that the police dealt with evidence requests, bringing them more into line with other countries' approaches. Such a change would also have had an effect on all other financial organisations that dealt with that country's police, as well as the country's regulator, prosecuting authorities and even the law courts. Tightening up in this way may have deterred criminals from targeting this particular country for money laundering. The lessons learned had the potential for a system-wide impact.

A lessons-learned session could extend to any level of learning, from implementing, through improving to innovating. For teams to achieve innovative learning, time needs to be invested into the learning process to identify and challenge the assumptions and then to open up new ways of thinking. Unfortunately, even though many of the conditions for innovative learning existed at the time, George's team chose not to invest time in learning deeply because he was moving on. Therefore, learning only reached implementing level.

I hope, as people read this book and have chances to stimulate learning better, together within their Extra-Dependent Teams using techniques I have shared, or indeed techniques of their own, that examples might be generated of innovative learning that favourably impacts the wider system of Inter-Dependent Teams across and perhaps even beyond the organisation.

But for managers to be able to stimulate such learning, it is likely that they will need to be more than just a manager. They will need to be a leader. When it comes to leading an Extra-Dependent Team the conventional model, which relies on a common goal, is inadequate. If an Extra-Dependent Team has no common goal, how can it be led?

Note

1 The takeaways are technically explicit knowledge, but they indicate a plan to internalise the knowledge in the action of applying it.

References

Argyris, C (1994) Good communication that blocks learning. *Harvard Business Review*, July–August, 77–85.

Boydell, T and Leary, M (1996) *Identifying training needs*, Institute of Personnel and Development, London.

Downey, M (2003) *Effective Coaching: Lessons from the Coaches' Coach*, 3rd Ed., Cengage Learning, Boston, MA.

Hawkins, P (2011) *Leadership Team Coaching: Developing Collective Transformational Leadership*, Kogan Page, London.

Hawkins, P (ed.) (2014) *Leadership Team Coaching in Practice*, Kogan Page, London.

Hawkins, P and Smith, N (2006) *Coaching, Mentoring and Organizational Consultancy: Supervision and Development*, Maidenhead: Open University Press.

Katzenbach, J and Smith, D (1993) *The Wisdom of Teams: Creating the High-Performance Organization*, Harvard Business School Press, Harvard, MA.

NHS England (2014) MDT development: Working toward an effective multidisciplinary/multiagency team, NHS England, 7 January, www.england.nhs.uk/wp-content/uploads/2015/01/mdt-dev-guid-flat-fin.pdf

Nonaka, I and Takeuchi, H (1995) *The Knowledge-Creating Company: How Japanese Companies Create the Dynamics of Innovation*, Oxford University Press, Oxford.

Pedler, M (2008) *Action Learning for Managers*, Gower Publishing, Farnham.

Revans, R W (1982) *The Origins and Growth of Action Learning*, Chartwell-Bratt, Lund.

Thornton, C (2016) *Group and Team Coaching: The Secret Life of Groups*, Routledge, London.

9 Extra-Dependent Team leadership

So far in this book we have accepted that Extra-Dependent Teams are formally managed and have explored how the manager can understand, appreciate and develop the team differently as a result. But as I highlighted in Chapter 3, managers aspire to be seen as leaders and they are expected to be leaders by their organisations. But is it possible to lead an Extra-Dependent Team? Is leadership only the stuff of Inter-Dependent Teams? I don't believe that organisations that require greater productivity and engagement from their staff in order to survive in our increasingly complex world, can afford to tolerate managers that don't add the sort of value that a high-performing Extra-Dependent Team can offer. They need leaders. Managers, not employees, are often the source of many of the engagement issues that organisations struggle to address. Indeed, I have highlighted many examples already where the actions of managers *prevent* the development of teams but reinforce their own authoritarian power. Teams should be engaging places where people can feel a sense of belonging, progression and wellbeing. I believe that leadership has a vital part to play in achieving such prosperous environments.

But what part does leadership play in Extra-Dependent Teams? This is a challenging question to address because the traditional view of leadership actually reinforces the conventional view of teams. So to recognise leadership within an Extra-Dependent Team requires us to reframe our understanding of leadership.

Traditional leadership

The traditional view of leadership in organisations is of a 'hero' figure that is an important, senior (typically male) strategist, who overcomes all the odds, including resistance by employees, by wielding power through their control of resources to deliver an outcome. This traditional view has been challenged for many years and is still being challenged today (Meindl et al., 1985; Mintzberg, 2004; Haslam et al., 2011; McChrystal et al., 2015; Hawkins, 2017). The traditional view is clearly still very strong in the minds of managers in organisations or these attempts to reframe leadership would have been more successful and writers would have stopped having to make this point.

Perhaps the reason for this is captured in how we define leadership. According to Gary Yukl, most definitions of leadership share the assumption that it involves an influence process concerned with facilitating, 'the performance of a collective task' (Yukl, 2002, p. 19). If this is the case, then the conventional view of teams mutually reinforces the traditional view of leaders: working together to achieve a common goal. Since the conventional mental model of teams is around combining difference, it implies that a leader needs to provide something *different* to the team to be of value. The difference that the leader is expected to bring to a team continues to reflect the traditional view of leadership and thus continues to reinforce the traditional view. As one of the leading proponents of the Team School states: 'You are the team leader. Achieving clarity means being insistent and unapologetic about exercising your authority to specify your team's purpose' (Wageman et al., 2008, p. 75). For Inter-Dependent Teams, therefore, the role of leader is to be different *in order* for the team to work together to achieve a common goal. But within an Extra-Dependent Team, where team members don't work together and their combination is based on similarity, then what is leadership? And what value does it add? If Extra-Dependent Teams don't have a common goal, how can they be led?

To understand the leadership of similarity is to understand how to appreciate, affect and steer the strong bond of Extra-Dependent Teams. We need to return to social identity theory.

From me to we

In their award-winning book, *The New Psychology of Leadership*, Haslam et al. (2011) use comprehensive research and a range of other evidence to provide a compelling alternative to the heroic definition of leadership. They critique the traditional view as too individualistic which completely overlooks the part played by followers. The traditional view appears to see leaders and leadership as one and the same when, they argue, leadership is a *verb* rather than a noun; leaders describe a person; leader*ship* describes a relationship process. Leadership therefore *requires* followers. After all, what is a leader if they have no followers? They reject the tradition of 'me-ness' and subsequently researched the leadership of 'we-ness'.

Their research on leadership culminated in a radical thesis on leadership that revolves around shared identity. For understanding Extra-Dependent Teams, it proves a compelling way to realise the value of leadership within a team where there is no common goal. They suggest four leadership principles which I relate to Extra-Dependent Teams as follows:

- *Being one of us* – leaders as one of the team.
- *Doing it for us* – leaders as champions of the team.

- *Crafting a sense of us* – leaders as skilled entrepreneurs of team identity.
- *Making us matter* – leaders as embedders of team reputation.

For our purposes, the first two principles focus on a leader being able to represent the Extra-Dependent Team. The second two principles focus on the leader transforming what the team means to the wider system.

Being one of us

An Extra-Dependent Team manager first needs to be seen as 'one of us' rather than 'one of them'. This harks back to the notion of comparative fit that was introduced in Chapter 4 – comparison *between* 'in-group' and 'out-group' relative to the wider context. The team needs to identify similarity with the manager, they can't see the manager as too different. This is one of the reasons why Extra-Dependent Team managers are typically player/managers where they practise as well as manage what the team does. For instance, a sales manager needs to have a background in sales or a head of engineering needs to be an engineer. If they don't have this basic shared identity they aren't credible in the eyes of the team.

Leading from the Periphery

If the team manager is perceived as 'one of them' rather than 'one of us' by the Extra-Dependent Team, the manager is immediately placed within the Periphery layer. For instance, in an Extra-Dependent Team of project managers I helped develop within a global legal firm, the manager often described herself as a lawyer rather than a project manager because she was in an interim role and that was how she saw herself. For the team members, this immediately distanced her from them as they all had project management backgrounds. As Haslam et al. state, 'would-be leaders' primary goal should not be to differentiate themselves from those they seek to lead, but rather to emphasize their commonalities' (2011, p. 106). When I discussed the dynamics of the team with the manager, she plotted herself at the Periphery layer. It is very difficult to manage a team from the periphery without having a rapid, inbound trajectory.

Without being seen as 'one of us' the manager found it difficult to persuade the team members to change, something that the team's stakeholders were pressuring the manager to do, and the driver for the team development. During one meeting the whole team explored the Extra-Dependent Team dynamics together. During the discussion the manager made it clear that as an experienced lawyer in the firm she had run many, many legal projects in the past. She started to talk about herself more in terms of project management and less in terms of law. It completely changed the perception of the team and her credibility with them. Leaders, according to Haslam et al., are 'able to influence *and lead* others – sometimes in creative and unexpected ways – because, and to the extent that, they are seen by those others to represent what it is that "we" means and what it is that "we" stand for' (2011, p. 107). By emphasising her similarities, she had started to be seen to be part of the common practice, to have experience of the shared repertoire, of having a credible reputation in the business. At that point her trajectory changed course from being peripheral to being inbound. For the team, perhaps she was 'one of us' after all?

Leading from the Active layer

A new team leader on an inbound trajectory needs to quickly familiarise themselves with the existing shared repertoire that the team has. The manager will then enter the Active layer. Leading from the Active layer is also possible, but again, not ideal. As a very experienced engineer, Erik the engineering team manager (see Chapter 5) should have occupied the Core layer, but actually only occupied the Active layer. He was seen by the team to be divorced from the engineering activity and focused instead on 'management' issues (i.e. 'them') such as recruitment. It weakened his position as a leader within the team. But he had compensated for this by developing a strong relationship with the Core member Tony, who was the de facto leader within the team. It meant that during a team meeting, when Tony openly praised Erik for the quality of the engineering recruits Erik had brought into the wider engineering function, the respect and gratitude Tony showed enabled Erik to be more strongly seen as 'one of us' within the team.

Leading from the Core

Ideally, the manager needs to occupy the Core layer of the Extra-Dependent Team to lead convincingly, and not simply by association as Erik did. They need to be identified as a role model by other team members. In the Core they are able to demonstrate their mastery of the shared repertoire and their ability to represent the combined capability. Here we must return to the topic of normative fit as introduced in Chapter 4 – where those *within* a particular in-group talk and act in a way the members of the in-group might expect. For a leader to be in the Core layer, the others in the team need to recognise them as a *prototype* of the common practice – an exemplar version. Not only does a leader need to be seen as 'one of us' to be in the Core layer, leaders must be recognised, 'as epitomizing the nature of the group that is to be led. To be a leader, one must be seen to speak not for "me" (nor for "them"), but for the very essence of "*us*"' (Haslam et al., 2011, p. 108, emphasis in original).

But Haslam et al. provide a health warning. 'Leaders can be ahead of the group, but never so far ahead that they are out there on their own' (Haslam et al., 2011, p. 106). Leaders in the Core must therefore not be isolated. Such a situation would be akin to the team identity outlined in Chapter 5, called

Cult. When this happens the *leader* becomes the bond for the team, rather than the common practice. In which case the focus is not on delivery of performance outside the team, but rather on devotion inwards, towards the leader. The team might convince itself that it is doing well, but it would have a poor reputation as its performance would not reflect what the wider organisation needs from it.

Doing it for us

Being 'one of us' is only the starting point for leadership. The leader needs to be recognised as able to do something for the team's identity, too. When Malinda became head of risk she established her credibility early on because she had a pedigree background in risk management, albeit as a consultant to other industries. She quickly learned the shared repertoire and got directly involved in the work of the team. Yet many elder team members grumbled about her focus on following rigid risk processes. For them, risk involved a great deal more tacit knowledge than the explicit knowledge that consultants talked about.

On the first day of a two-day team meeting, a review was conducted of a particularly challenging period where each regional risk manager had had a particularly tough time with their respective regional directors over a major review of why the organisation was still delivering late and over budget. During the discussion Malinda won over some of her fiercest critics when she started to share insights about some of her own tough conversations with senior managers, putting herself on the line for the work of the team. This was new information for the team and it shifted their perspective of her. To the team, it was clear that Malinda stood for more than just following process. She had managed to influence senior management in a manner that the regional risk managers struggled with in their regions. But more than that, the team could also see that Malinda was championing risk management and the team's importance within the organisation. In the regional risk manager's eyes, she was becoming an in-group champion. She was respecting and promoting their combined capability, and as a result the team was giving her respect in return.

Respect is a vital contributor to the ability to lead an Extra-Dependent Team as it enhances collective self-esteem, increases rule compliance, increases citizenship behaviour (i.e. putting oneself out for fellow members) and increases commitment to the group (Haslam et al., 2011). But Malinda needed to do more to be seen to be 'doing it for us'. Malinda had created an opportunity through her disclosure to move the team forward. Day 2 of the team meeting would need much more learning together before the team could feel aligned.

On day 2 I asked Malinda to share her 'target state' – a term she had used a number of times to describe strategic changes she wanted to make. I thought she might want to create a common goal but actually she described a desired change in the relationship the team had with the rest of the organisation. As she articulated what she wanted, I wrote it on a flip chart:

* We decide what good looks like [with regard to risk management].
* We have a role to drive [risk] maturity – i.e. ongoing education, continuous capability development, mentoring.
* We provide specialist support [as opposed to basic risk management].
* We provide assurance that has a performance benefit.
* We proactively provide that assurance to regional directors.
* We have senior management agreement.
* We have consistency.

For alignment to this target state, the team needed to learn together what it actually meant. For learning to occur, the team needed to discuss it constructively. The question at this point was therefore not, 'Do you agree?', because it would have split the team immediately. Instead, the learning needed to share opinions about the benefits of such an end state.

The question was then asked, 'What value will that target state allow this team to provide?'

Informally we did a 'round' hearing everyone's answers to this question and not leaving anyone out, or assuming the first answer was either the correct one or the best one. Everyone was starting to explore the target state together – they started to align. Each and every contribution was captured:

The value that this target state will give us will be:

* Improved decision making by giving assurance that risk is fully understood.
* Transfer of accountability to the teams that are accountable.
* Capacity to provide more in-depth specialism where it is most needed.
* To give greater confidence to the teams to deliver their performance.
* To gather evidence to prove we are as safe as we say we are.
* An economy of effort – we are cheaper (more valuable).
* To provide a joined-up picture of all control systems.
* To ensure resources (all) are used effectively.
* An improved work/life balance through clearer priorities.
* For this to become business as usual.
* To ensure that [risk management] is done!
* To achieve greater stakeholder confidence.
* To be better able to streamline the team.
* To assist in deliverability, affordability and being readily available.
* To be more able to assure.
* To be able to identify future trends and flag up potential future issues.
* For the team to become more insightful, better skilled and more expert.
* To drive risk maturity and risk culture throughout the business.

The length of the list demonstrated the shift the whole team had taken. They had stopped arguing amongst themselves about the issues of the past and had started to recognise what the future could look like for the team. The combination of Malinda's tough stance with her senior managers and an end state that the whole team saw as having wide-ranging value for them personally and for what 'we' do meant that Malinda was seen to be 'doing it for us'.

But 'being one of us' and 'doing it for us' is simply not enough to truly lead an Extra-Dependent Team. Leaders also need to project the essence of the team across the wider system so that stakeholders realise the value of the team. The third and fourth leadership principles therefore explain the importance of transforming the nature of how the team participates within the wider system and ensuring that the contribution of the team matters. This is a much greater challenge that managers of Extra-Dependent Teams need to grapple with if they are to be identified as real leaders.

Crafting a sense of us

Leaders aren't just participants in the status quo. They are directly involved in shaping our world view and, with it, changing social reality. With us and through us, leaders are able to transform our sense of selves so that we are mobilised towards a different future than the one we would otherwise head towards. So where once we might have seen limitations, leaders enable us to see possibilities.

To influence in this way Haslam et al. contend that leaders craft a sense of us around three dimensions:

- the source – who can mobilise us?
- the target – who is mobilised?
- the content – what is the nature of mobilisation?

In our understanding of Extra-Dependent Teams, this might more clearly be defined as a shift in common practice. Figure 9.1 is a simple way to understand this by recognising a shift in the layers of the team:

Figure 9.1 shows two overlapping sets of layers in an Extra-Dependent Team. The solid line indicates the present common practice. The dotted line indicates a potential, future common practice. This future common practice is offset compared to the present indicating that:

- where the present doesn't overlap with the future, shared repertoire will be lost; and
- where the future doesn't overlap with the present, shared repertoire will be gained.

The source is identified as the leader, the person influencing the common practice. In the present they are Core, but not as prototypical as other Core

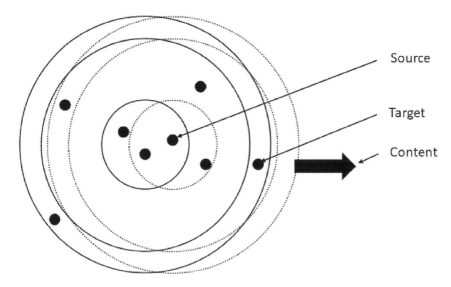

Figure 9.1 Transforming the common practice.

members. In the future common practice, the leader is much more central and therefore much more prototypical. They therefore embody the future sense of 'us' by the way they talk and act, how these are mirrored in their achievements on behalf of the team and by the stories that are chosen to be told about them.

The target of the influence is the rest of the team. It is clear that there is much movement within the team. With the shift in the future common practice, a Core member can be demoted to Active member, whilst an Active member could be promoted to Core member. These represent learning trajectories relative to the shift in common practice as Core members fail to learn the developing practice, whilst Active members might have been promoting it for some time, but it had yet to be accepted as role model behaviour. In effect, the inbound trajectory for these Active members is less about them moving towards the Core and more about the Core shifting in favour of them because of their modelling of the leader's shared repertoire. Elsewhere in the common practice some Active members remain Active members whilst others are demoted to Peripheral, and some Peripheral members leave the team, unable to shift their individual repertoire to match the shifting shared repertoire of the team.

The content of the influence is the shift in common practice including a shift in shared repertoire (learning different skills, selecting different stories, changing standards, bringing on new equipment), a shift in combined capability (an improvement in performance) and a shift in reputation (a different sense of 'us'). For the leader to make this identity shift, they need to be the change they wish to see, to be able to articulate *and* demonstrate *and* achieve progress towards that future state. There is inevitably a degree of tension between those who wish to maintain the current common practice and the leader who is intent on shifting towards a future (and different) common practice.

But in Extra-Dependent Teams leadership at this level cannot be restricted to the team itself. Because the work of the team is done elsewhere in the organisation and for the leader to be associated with the success of this activity, the leader must acknowledge that their target must also include 'them', other members of other teams elsewhere in the organisation, even beyond into other organisations. The leader therefore needs to have eyes on the wider world, giving consideration beyond the boundaries of the Extra-Dependent Team and into the Inter-Dependent Teams within which the team members operate. The leader is paying attention to the effect the Extra-Dependent Team's combined capability has elsewhere in the organisational system. In doing so, leaders that support the integration of the Extra-Dependent Team's work to enhance the performance of the Inter-Dependent Teams ensure that the sense of 'us' is *with* 'them' *rather than against* 'them'.

To work with 'them' the leader needs to recognise that their leadership 'footprint' is greater than the boundaries of the Extra-Dependent Team. They need to recognise that they have a strategic responsibility to influence across the system. To do this, they need to increase their level of abstraction (see Chapter 4) and craft the identity of the team so that it can be seen as 'us' by the rest of the organisation. Crafting involves shaping the shared repertoire towards the future common practice. It's not just about changing processes or revising job descriptions. It's about the way that this is done, the language used, the imagery created, the metaphors explored, the actions taken.

An example of this played out within Malinda's risk team. Having shared her 'target state' with the team and them having identified value for themselves in it, there was a need to develop new words and new ways of relating with key stakeholders in the regions so that they could start to make the changes desired. The team's shared repertoire would have to shift towards a new practice that none had done before. The team would have to innovate and the leader would have to redefine what it meant to be 'us' within the wider organisational system.

At an event where all the team were present, the team had to find a way of learning together to shift their shared repertoire, in particular with regard to the way they related to people outside the team. They identified two priority stakeholders that were crucial to this relationship shift: regional directors and project managers. The team needed to rehearse how to speak differently with them. We started with the regional director. We ran an exercise where, in pairs, with little preparation, they did an elevator pitch of one minute to each other imagining that the other person was their respective regional director. The limited preparation time was deliberate to help them develop this pitch through several iterations, not get it right first time. This was all about learning better together. It wasn't about proving to each other but improving with each other. Each pair would hear two versions – their own and their partner's – so that when partners were switched each person could combine the best and practice again, learning and improving each time. A third switch was done, so after about six minutes they had heard three other people's versions and practised and altered their own three times.

Back together all the pitches were shared so that everyone could hear the consistencies or inconsistencies of the shared repertoire. Each one was slightly different but a brief discussion identified that the reasons for these differences were actually consistent – each regional director had to be dealt with individually, touching the agenda items most important to them. It was clear evidence that the team was starting to understand their influence was not within the team, but that their sense of 'we-ness' had to include many people outside the team.

Instead of stopping there, a similar activity was run to learn how each regional risk manager could win over the toughest of project managers. A 'role play' scenario was improvised and a member of the team was selected to play a particularly negative project manager. Other team members would then take it in turns to role play the scenario of influencing the project manager around this new relationship. As each team member tried and got so far, other team members stepped in to take their place, with each one trying different techniques to make progress with the conversation. Everyone watched as Core, Active and Peripheral members tried it out. Everyone learned. The techniques that made the most progress were highlighted, practised again and reinforced. This was an act of externalising tacit knowledge from multiple team members. Rehearsal allowed for internalisation and the whole process was steeped in socialisation as the team learned to learn together.

The team had together crafted new shared repertoire that they could each use to start to make a shift in their reputation. Because if their new relationship was to make any sort of difference to the rest of the organisation, the team would recognise that they mattered to the regions.

Making us matter

This last principle of leadership builds on the previous three. At this level the leader has achieved a relationship with people inside and outside the Extra-Dependent Team that acknowledge the importance and contribution of the team as part of the efforts of a wider whole. In other words, the leader is operating at the system level, playing an influential part in releasing the full potential of the team in conjunction with everyone else within the organisation.

This is why the third conversation in the performance management triangle (see Chapter 7) between the Extra-Dependent Team manager and the Inter-Dependent Team manager is so important. It is an opportunity to lead the embedding of the team into the future business of the organisation.

Embedding of the future common practice involves using the language of 'us', demonstrating what 'we' can do together and constructing materials, events, agreements, spaces or routines that embed the combined capability of the team into the broader value of the organisation. When the team innovates its shared repertoire it can only deploy additional capability into the rest of the organisation when the rest of the organisation is able to accommodate it. It is pointless developing new techniques if the Inter-Dependent Teams that use them aren't in a position to do so. It means the Extra-Dependent Team leader needs to continuously communicate, challenge, shape and listen to stakeholders within the wider system so that the new combined capability has a part to play and the new value of the team can be realised. Then the team is adding strategic value, enough to impact the marketplace.

But in my experience, Extra-Dependent Teams consider themselves too peripheral for this – they refer to 'the business' or 'the core business' or just 'them', thus distancing themselves from the very people they seek to influence. Similarly, they have a tendency to articulate their contribution as compulsory, thereby emphasising their separation from the core purpose of the organisation. For instance, the engineers were *legally* required for construction, the anti-money-laundering team were a regulatory requirement and the matrons were a nationally created role that the hospital had to accept locally. Finally, in my experience, managers of Extra-Dependent Teams have a tendency to change jobs quite often. Perhaps it's the stress of herding cats, perhaps it's critical instances such as George's, perhaps it's something else. But it is difficult to achieve leadership that makes us matter if the manager keeps changing.

Malinda too chose to move on – for her health as much as anything else. But if she were to stay she could have made the team matter within each region by communicating regularly with the regional directors, articulating the team's future combined capability (end state) and understanding the future demands and issues that were common across the regions. Just by meeting them, engaging with them and listening to them she would demonstrate the future relationship that her team was trying to create. Through building her relationship she could oversee the permanent changes to procedures, behaviours, events and agreements that would embed the value of the team into the routine work of the regions. Each regional risk manager would know that they really mattered, because each region would be routinely delivering projects on time and on budget.

References

Haslam, S A, Reicher, S D and Platow, M J (2011) *The New Psychology of Leadership: Identity, Influence and Power*, Psychology Press, Hove.

Hawkins, P (2017) *Tomorrow's Leadership and the Necessary Revolution in Today's Leadership Development*, Henley Business School, Reading.

McChrystal, S, Collins, T, Silverman, D and Fussell, C (2015) *Team of Teams: New Rules of Engagement for a Complex World*, Penguin, New York.

Meindl, J R, Ehrlich, S B and Dukerich, J M (1985) The romance of leadership. *Administrative Science Quarterly*, 30, 78–102.

Mintzberg, H (2004) *Managers not MBAs*, Pearson, Harlow.

Wageman, R, Nunes, D A, Burruss, J A and Hackman, J R (2008) *Senior Leadership Teams*, Harvard Business School Press, Harvard, MA.

Yukl, G (2002) *Leadership in Organizations*, Prentice-Hall, Upper Saddle River, NJ.

Part III

10 Reflection on practice

I have chosen to use this final chapter to reflect on my own practice. The first idea I had for Extra-Dependent Teams came as early as 2006, albeit that isn't the language I used. That's over ten years ago and my thinking and practice have both moved forward considerably since then. As with any practice, mine has been part of multiple communities that have helped me to develop and experiment with my original ideas, shaping them, honing them, solidifying them. To complete this book, I reflect on my practice from the perspective of each of these communities of practice in turn, highlighting what made me a member and what I learned through participation that is relevant to this book. As you read, I hope that you too will reflect on what it means to be a member of the community of practice of Extra-Dependent Teams.

The community of practice of being in Inter-Dependent Teams

I have been a member of many, many different teams, often in a leadership capacity. At 13 years old I was leading a team of six peers on overnight hikes on Dartmoor. At 16 I was voted to become chairman of my Venture Scout Unit. At 22 years old I was leading a team of paratroopers on patrols in Northern Ireland during heightened tensions in 1992.

Each of these experiences helped me understand the importance of how teams work. For instance, in Northern Ireland we patrolled in an Inter-Dependent Team of 12 soldiers in a formation made up of three sub-teams of four soldiers. Our common goal was two-fold: to prevent terrorist activity and to get everyone back in one piece. Everyone in the patrol needed everyone else. Each sub-team was a mix of different capabilities including a sub-team commander, a medium-machine gunner, a rifleman and a light-machine gunner. The three sub-teams would provide mutual support by operating approximately 100–300 metres away from each other. Spread out, it was difficult to attack all three sub-teams at once, giving the ability to defend ourselves more dynamically. Everyone therefore depended on everyone else. When an incident did occur, as they sporadically did, we were as ready as we could be to achieve our common goal and prevent terrorist activity and get back in one piece. This experience alone was enough to appreciate the importance and the methods of conventional teams.

We learned to savour team success when we interrupted an IRA cell setting up to shoot down the very helicopter we were in. Yet we also experienced the worst of teams when two lance corporals drowned whilst swimming across a river that the rest of the team crossed via a bridge as planned. Common goals are so important to Inter-Dependent Teams. We had succeeded in one and failed in the other.

More recently I took up the opportunity of leading the executive committee of a local charity. The charity needed a new building and it was clearly a common goal for which the executive committee needed to become an Inter-Dependent Team. I set to work building a team of difference from the people on the committee as well as additional specialists necessary for the common goal ahead. Each person had a different role – architect, building construction, fundraising (grants), fundraising (events), finance, operational continuity (keeping the charity going whilst the old building was taken down and a new one built), grounds, decorations and furnishing. I put myself in charge of coordination. No one had the same role. Difference was everything. With everyone knowing their part, we all worked together to achieve our common goal – a new building. We achieved it and, compared to other similar charities, did it in record time. In ten months we had gone from submitting planning permission to opening our new building. During this time we raised and spent £250,000 and demolished and rebuilt on the same site. At no point had our charity work been negatively affected. It was hard work and all voluntary. But it was an amazing experience which everyone remembers with pride and the new building is very successful.

Experiences such as this reinforced my belief in the Team School and how powerful the key lessons are to learn about how to lead such teams. But I have also been a member of other communities of practice and they too have been important to me.

The community of practice of communities of practice

I was introduced to the concept of communities of practice whilst on a master's degree course in management and organisational learning at Lancaster University Management School in 1998–9. The Department of Management Learning that ran the course had a fabulous reputation for research, new thinking and cutting-edge practice and the course itself was revolutionary in my eyes. For instance, we drove our own learning process, choosing what we wanted to focus on, co-creating experiential learning with some colleagues and then sharing it with others so that everyone was learning together. It was action learning in the loosest and most invigorating sense of the term.

We selected our own topics to write our graded essays on. Not only that, but we decided what the title should be and, best of all, we marked our own papers! Actually, in our learning groups of (typically) four people we all marked each other's papers, including our own, before having a discussion about them as a group with our tutor, finally deciding the mark collaboratively. It was radical and it felt liberating from the didactic training I'd experienced in the army.

Many of the sources of my inspirations came during this year, including a relatively new idea called communities of practice. It appealed to me in the way that Wenger himself describes communities of practice: 'It has both the eye-opening character of novelty and the forgotten familiarity of obviousness' (Wenger, 1998, p. 7).

Communities of practice appeared to reflect so much of what we were doing on the course. We were a community, we learned together and our practice was in achieving an MA in organisational learning. Yet we had to perform individually. We were accountable for our own coursework and if one person failed it would not stop anyone else from succeeding. It was a hugely rewarding process, but a completely different experience from being in a team. I recognised this difference and valued it. I wanted to use it elsewhere.

Beyond this experience I have found that it is uncommon for people to be aware of communities of practice, but everyone is likely to be a member of one, even if they don't know it. More than that, I have found that those who do talk about communities of practice often know little about them beyond the name itself. I have found this disappointing as I thought I was a Peripheral member to a mature community of practitioners. What I have come to realise is that I am probably an Active member, perhaps even Core.

When researching the dynamics in Extra-Dependent Teams, I set up a community of practice consisting of independent consultants. The idea was to run it over eight meetings during a six-month period. Everyone who was invited to join did much the same thing, but no one depended on anyone else. Learning was maximised during the day-long meetings and the agenda was collaboratively defined.

I learned a great deal from that experience, including how much time it takes to feel comfortable enough to discuss the really valuable stuff, how initially people looked for knowledge 'outside' the group (i.e. referring to books, etc.), but also that the real richness comes from sharing experience, challenging practice and keeping a focus on taking real action. I called it DidCOP, named after fusing the location (Didcot in Oxfordshire) with the pneumonic for community of practice. Five years after starting it up, it is still continuing.

The DidCOP experiment was a major encouragement for me, not only because it road tested my learning on communities of practice, but also because I was urged by my fellow members to pursue my thinking on Extra-Dependent Teams further.

The community of practice of team development

As someone who had experience of being in teams and leading teams, I chose to develop other teams as a consultant. Indeed, I was a member of Steve's team in Chapter 1. I was one of the consultants who worked with clients to develop their leaders and their teams. I was also present during the team development day when we diagnosed ourselves as being a working group.

But on the train home I reflected on the definition of team that we had been using and realised that the consultant team would *never* meet that definition. A simultaneous thought jumped into my head which excited me: the idea that the team might be better to consider itself a *community of practice*. After all, I had thrived in a community of practice in the recent past and found it very rewarding. So the first thing I did on getting home was to write an email to Steve. I was really excited to tell him my idea and the sooner I did so, I thought, the sooner we could all develop as a community of practice rather than as a team.

What happened next confused me at first. Steve didn't know what a community of practice was, nor had he ever heard of one. What he'd done with my email was to pass it on to two of the *senior* consultants (I was just a consultant) in the team for their opinion. I had huge respect for both senior consultants and had learned a great deal from them during my time in the team. But they hadn't heard of communities of practice either. My suggestion got no support and it rapidly died a death.

Sometime later I reflected back on this situation and realised that I was an Active member with new ideas that challenged the team, and the two senior consultants were the elders in the Core who were deciding how the shared repertoire would be developed. What's more, because the manager was a newcomer on a slow inbound trajectory, he was in no position to support me: he relied on the experience of the elders. It was an important moment for me as I noted how the theory I was developing was helping to explain my own experience of developing that very theory. It enthused me to understand it and develop it more. It was through this experience that I appreciated the importance of the elders' role to listen to newcomers, just as much as newcomers have a role to listen to elders.

The community of practice of research

After the consulting team's demise I set up my own development business where I had the freedom to research my thinking further. I started reading at first, believing that I was still playing catch-up in an area of knowledge in which others were expert. I started to study more about teams and communities of practice. I read a lot on teams and communities of practice to improve my knowledge, most notably Wenger (1998), McDermott and Archibald (2010), Katzenbach and Smith (1993), Hawkins and Smith (2006), Pedler (2008) and Hackman and Wageman. I even read Tuckman (1965), which proved very enlightening, but not as I had expected.

I developed some initial ideas and started to test them out. Erik's engineering team was one of my first experiments. In return for pro bono coaching of Erik, he and his boss allowed me to observe team meetings and develop different techniques to experiment with. One early technique I tested was the dynamics of learning trajectories and layers which were a direct pull from Wenger's work. Wenger identified these within communities of practice, but would they also be observable within a managed team?

I tested this out by watching the dynamics in a team meeting and then plotting the team's layers and trajectories. After the meeting I explained the theory of the dynamics to Erik before asking him to plot each team member one at a time. He chose who to go with first and then positioned that team member. We would then discuss his thinking before I shared what I thought and we discussed it again. What was surprising was how similar we both were with our assessment, including of Erik's own position. It gave me huge comfort that an intact team was behaving like a community of practice. Not only that, it prompted new thinking for Erik about Jack, the elder on the Periphery, who Erik found so difficult to manage. It was a breakthrough for Erik's management of Jack and one for me in my pursuit of my thinking. The dynamics were identifiable, even to a novice, and they proved a new way of explaining what was going on in the team and very useful in indicating what action might be taken to move the team forward.

Now I have to admit that studying the philosophical underpinnings of knowledge such as ontology (the nature of knowledge), epistemology (our association with knowledge) and methodology (how we choose to enquire into knowledge) during my master's degree and for anyone reading this who is an Active, Core or elder in the community of practice of academic research, I am aware that I have followed a very loose version of action research. But I am also aware that I am open to heavy critique at every step because my research was not written down or methodical. But I am not aiming for a PhD, nor do I want to be an academic. As a practitioner I am very pleased with my years of practical testing and experimenting and continue to be enthusiastic about it as it continues to serve those who experience it well. But in the community of practice of research, I remain a Peripheral member.

The community of practice of Extra-Dependent Teams

Through my research and experimenting I was realising that I was breaking new ground. This was an area of interest, thinking and practice that no one else was operating in. I realised that I needed to develop my own repertoire. At the top of the list was language around what I was trying to explain. The terms *teams* and *communities of practice* just seemed to conjure fixed beliefs about how things ought to work. Whenever I used these terms with people they were too inconsistent in stimulating a constructive response which I believed my work was due. I was finding the conventional mental model of teams too ridged and at the same time too vague. It seemed everyone wanted everything to be a team. I needed new terms that helped both types of team to be equally attractive. As it was, whenever I said to a manager that they managed a community of practice rather than a team, they smiled and continued to argue why their team was a team (even though they wanted help with it because it didn't work like a team should!). Erik initially responded in this way, and others after him also did. I needed to develop my language.

At first I was inspired by the connections the idea had with the organisational matrix and so I trialled 'horizontal' and 'vertical' teams. But it was clear that what was vertical in one organisation was horizontal in another. It just wouldn't be clear. So I came up with 'odds' versus 'evens', the former being the difference of teams and the latter being the similarity of communities of practice. I really liked this because I thought people would be more likely to want to be 'even' than 'odd'. Some people liked it, a few didn't. Enough people indicated to me that that the word 'odd' would potentially be too damaging for people. So I decided to scrap it.

Finally, I came up with inter-dependent for teams and just needed to finalise the opposite. Intra-dependent sounded too similar and was likely to confuse. So I came up with extra-dependent. I liked it because it was totally new and seemed to easily describe some of the key features of the two teams. I realised there were some risks – extra-dependent might mean that there was *more* dependency, for instance – but I felt happy enough and I had to settle on something. Since then only a few people have challenged these terms, but never vigorously. So they are now fixed. The final step was to ensure that the words were distinctive enough for readers to know that I was referring to something specific rather than what they wanted them to mean. And so I capitalised and hyphenated them to make them stand out. The bare essentials of the shared repertoire would be the names Inter-Dependent and Extra-Dependent Teams.

More liberation of language followed. The more I experimented with Extra-Dependent Teams, the more I recognised the need to alter the language of Wenger and others in order to help shape a new shared repertoire for a community of practice of Extra-Dependent Teams. Chief amongst these was my development of the words and meanings of the terms elders, newcomers, shared repertoire, combined capability and reputation. I only sought to alter language where the original didn't sufficiently match what I was witnessing in my experiments. Yet I was urged on by Wenger's notion of reification and the part he identifies in how the development of language supports the development of practice and vice versa. Changing the language enabled me to reframe the practice I was experimenting with and to find new meaning in it.

Finally, I found very little written on leadership in communities of practice. And yet, for an intact team, I knew that the manager would need to lead. It was then I realised that the work of Social Identity Theory provided a compelling angle on this which supported Extra-Dependent Teams for what they were, rather than trying to make them and their leaders something else. It was the final part of the jigsaw.

The more I developed my thinking and practice the more I realised that I was breaking away from the communities of practice of both teams and communities of practice. Indeed, the further I developed my thinking, the more I distanced myself from the Core and Active members of these communities. I realised that I was on a different learning trajectory compared to my colleagues within these existing communities of practice that was certainly not inbound but neither was it entirely outbound.

Reflection on my practice suggested to me that there might be a new trajectory that I was experiencing and which would be worth noting. Such a trajectory would involve tremendous learning but not towards the Core of the current community of practice. Instead, the learning would be towards a new Core, perhaps for a community of practice of the future. I mapped such a trajectory onto the layers (see Figure 10.1) and defined it as *rogue*. The features of such a trajectory are a deliberate pursuit of developed practice, but one that is out of step with the conventional practice and those who role model it.

I then realised I saw this in Extra-Dependent Teams a great deal, especially when it came to leadership. Leaders tried to shift the practice from a current context to a new one. When they did this it had a momentous impact on everyone in the team. This was when I realised that reusing the layers to map a current and future state of the team could help leaders and team members understand how each person was being affected differently by the changes the leader was introducing. It could then provide new solutions for leaders and help them develop the shared repertoire, combined capability and reputation to move the team from where it currently was to the new future state. The graphical representation of the leader's intent made it easier to have discussions with their team.

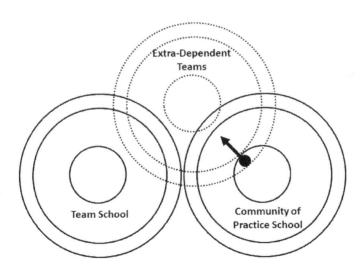

Figure 10.1 The rogue trajectory and developing a new community of practice.

Final reflections

I very nearly called this book *The Emperor's New Team*, using a play on words from the Hans Christian Anderson story, *The Emperor's New Clothes*. I nearly called it that because I have often felt like the small boy in the story who points out just what he sees, whilst everyone else is trying to see what they are told they 'ought' to see. Unlike the boy in the story who pointed out that the Emperor wasn't actually wearing clothes after all and got an immediate response from everyone around him, I have pointed this out to a number of different people and got a mix of some who recognised it and others who insisted on continuing to see what they wanted to. The first people I pointed it out to refused to see, but soon others were exclaiming to me, 'But that's obvious!' and 'You can't be the only one thinking like this, surely?'

I've no doubt that if you have read this far you will be a long way down the road of joining me in the Extra-Dependent Team community of practice. But others will have fallen well before you, giving up reading because it doesn't fit with their existing and firmly held mental model of teams. Indeed, if you feel the desire to share this book with someone who you believe will benefit from it, you might be disappointed in their response to it. They might not be as enthusiastic as perhaps you have been.

But don't be put off. I have learned to take these sorts of experiences and turn them into stories to tell – part of the shared repertoire of being in the community of practice of Extra-Dependent Teams. For me they are clear indications of which mental model the person uses. If such people are managers of Inter-Dependent Teams, it doesn't matter too much – their teams reflect that world view so everyone is fine. But if they are managers of an Extra-Dependent Team, then observe their actions, their frustrations and their problems. And once they are ready, return to them with that story and tempt them with an alternative world view, a plural mental model of teams. Help them to realise that there is another way to herd cats.

References

Hackman, R and Wageman, R (2001) *Top Teams: Why Some Work and Some Do Not*, Hay Group, Philadelphia, PA.

Hawkins, P and Smith, N (2006) *Coaching, Mentoring and Organizational Consultancy: Supervision and Development*, Open University Press, Maidenhead.

Katzenbach, J and Smith, D (1993) *The Wisdom of Teams: Creating the High-Performance Organization*, Harvard Business School Press, Harvard, MA.

McDermott, R and Archibald, D (2010) Harnessing Your Staff's Informal Networks, *Harvard Business Review*, March.

Pedler, M (2008) *Action Learning for Managers*, Gower, Padstow.

Tuckman, B W (1965) Developmental sequence in small groups. *Psychological Bulletin*, 63, 384–99.

Wenger, E (1998) *Communities of Practice: Learning, Meaning and Identity*, Cambridge University Press, New York.

Index

Printed in Great Britain
by Amazon

85572641R00099